Building Foundations: The Journey

Journey into the City of God
Building Foundations: A Spirit Filled Children's Church Curriculum

Tamera Kraft
Revival Fire 4 Kids Resource

M Zion Ridge Press LLC

Mt Zion Ridge Press LLC
295 Gum Springs Rd, NW
Georgetown, TN 37366

https://www.mtzionridgepress.com

Copyright © 2019 by Tamera Lynn Kraft
ISBN 13: 978-1-949564-45-7

Published in the United States of America
Publication Date: April 1, 2019

Editor-In-Chief: Michelle Levigne
Executive Editor: Tamera Lynn Kraft

Cover Art Copyright by Tamera Lynn Kraft and Mt Zion Ridge Press LLC © 2019

All rights reserved. No portion of this book may be reproduced or transmitted in any form or by any electronic or mechanical means, including photocopying, recording or by any information retrieval and storage system without permission of the publisher.

Ebooks, audiobooks, and print books are *not* transferrable, either in whole or in part. As the purchaser or otherwise *lawful* recipient of this book, you have the right to enjoy the novel on your own computer or other device. Further distribution, copying, sharing, gifting or uploading is illegal and violates United States Copyright laws.
Pirating of books is illegal. Criminal Copyright Infringement, *including* infringement without monetary gain, may be investigated by the Federal Bureau of Investigation and is punishable by up to five years in federal prison and a fine of up to $250,000.

Names, characters and incidents depicted in this book are products of the author's imagination, or are used in a fictitious situation. Any resemblances to actual events, locations, organizations, incidents or persons – living or dead – are coincidental and beyond the intent of the author.

Registration and Digital Files (Available for FREE with purchase of the curriculum): Digital files (jpeg graphics, video clips, other resources) are available to anyone who purchases and registers this curriculum at no additional cost. To register, click on this link http://eepurl.com/gIsELH or type it in the address box on your browser and fill out the form. We never sell or give away any information we receive.

DVD: If you prefer a DVD of Jpeg images and video clips, you may purchase it at http://mtzionridgepress.com for an additional cost.

The Journey includes these sections that can be bought and downloaded separately:

- **Part 1 –** *The Road* (5 lessons on the Romans Road of salvation)
- **Part 2 –** *The Bible: Your GPS for Life* (4 Lessons on how God's Word should guide your life)
  Part 3 – *City on a Hill* (4 lessons based on these scripture texts from the Sermon on the Mount about building a city on a hill – the kingdom of God in your life)

The Journey is available in PDF download and print. Each part of *The Journey* is available separately in PDF format only.

All Scripture in this curriculum is from the NIV (2011) Bible unless otherwise designated.

THE HOLY BIBLE, NEW INTERNATIONAL VERSION®, NIV® Copyright © 1973, 1978, 1984, 2011 by Biblica, Inc.® Used by permission. All rights reserved worldwide.

Some Scripture is also used from these versions:

THE HOLY BIBLE, INTERNATIONAL CHILDREN'S BIBLE® ICB Copyright© 1986, 1988, 1999, 2015 by Tommy Nelson™, a division of Thomas Nelson. Thomas Nelson is a registered trademark of HarperCollins Christian Publishing, Inc.

NEW KING JAMES VERSION® NKJV® Scripture taken from the New King James Version®. Copyright © 1982 by Thomas Nelson. Used by permission. All rights reserved.

The Journey © Mt Zion Ridge Press, 2019. All rights reserved.

Copyright permissions for this curriculum: When you register this curriculum, you are granted permission to make as many copies as needed for the use of the church or ministry registered only. ***Do not distribute this material to other churches or ministries without permission. Copying materials in any other way violates copyright laws.***

For questions about copyright issues or other matter concerning rights for this curriculum, contact revivalfire4kids@att.net.

Building Foundations Curriculum is a Revival Fire for Kids recourse. For more information about Revival Fire for Kids, check out their website at http://revivalfire4kids.net

Materials included:

The Road: 5 complete downloadable lessons including 10 object lessons, 10 skits, 8 games, 5 Bible Stories, 5 memory verse activities, and 5 small group discussions.

The Bible: Your GPS for Life: 4 complete downloadable lessons including 8 object lessons, 8 skits, 4 games, 4 Bible Stories, 4 memory verse activities, and 4 small group discussions.

City on a Hill©: 4 complete downloadable lessons including 8 object lessons, 8 skits, 4 games, 4 Bible Stories, 4 memory verse activities, and 4 small group discussions.

TABLE OF CONTENTS

How To Use This Curriculum:	pg 1
The Journey Part 1: The Road (The Romans Road)	3
Lesson 1: The Road Out of Eden	5
Lesson 2: The Wide Road and the Narrow Road.	13
Lesson 3: The Road to the Cross	21
Lesson 4: The Road to Damascus	31
Lesson 5: The Road to Rome	37
The Journey Part 2: The Bible: Your GPS for Life	43
Lesson 1: God's Word Guides Our Lives	45
Lesson 2: God's Word Points Us to Jesus	53
Lesson 3: God's Word Keeps Us from Sin	61
Lesson 4: Do What God's Word Says	67
The Journey Part 3: City on a Hill	73
Lesson 1: Our Foundation	75
Lesson 2: The Wise Builder	85
Lesson 3: Building Materials	93
Lesson 4: Letting Your Light Shine	101
About the Author	109

How To Use This Curriculum:

Scriptural Premise: The main theme for this curriculum is our journey with Christ. *The Road* teaches about salvation with the Romans Road theme and can be used evangelistically or as a guide to teach children how to witness. *The Bible: Your GPS for Life* teaches the importance of using the Bible as a guide for our lives and that the Bible is God's Word. *City on a Hill* teaches important principles on building the Kingdom of God in our lives.

Decorations: Decoration props and materials are not included with this curriculum. Decorations and set design can reflect building construction of a city with a road leading into the city. Road signs and maps can line the walls.

One suggestion is to use the road signs from *The Road*. You can also have saw horses and traffic cones. If you want to make a traffic light or buy a cardboard traffic light, that would add to the affect.

For the city buildings, you could use cardboard boxes from an appliance store and have someone in your church paint them to look like skyscrapers.

Another idea is to use a backdrop with a picture of a city or use the cover picture as a template for a backdrop. You can use any image included with this curriculum by projecting the image using a video projector onto a box or backdrop and drawing it. Use your creativity.

Italics: Italics are used for Scripture. They are also used in this curriculum for passages or speeches the teacher or worker may want to say in their own words. For skits, italics are only used to designate the person speaking.

Welcome:

Welcome: Each lesson will welcome the children with an introduction to that day's message.

Prayer: It's important to start each lesson with prayer.

Rules: A list of 5 Ups are included in the graphics available after registration. Rehearse the rules every week.

Theme Song: Get the kids up and moving at the beginning of every lesson with a fun theme song. Theme song that will work with this curriculum are *One Way* by Hillsong Kids or *Every Move I Make* by David Crowder.

Memory Verse: Every lesson has a memory verse. The verse will be included in a slide and will be illustrated in three ways. You can choose to use any of these illustrations to teach the verse, or you could use all three throughout your lesson.

Memory Verse Skit: A puppet or live skit with Peace Officer Shalom is included in each lesson to introduce the Memory Verse. The person doing the skit can dress in a police uniform. If you don't have access to a uniform, you can use blue pants, a blue shirt that buttons up the front with a badge and equipment you can buy at a discount or toy store. If a police officer attends you church, it would be great to recruit the officer for your skits and have the officer wear his uniform. You can also use a police officer puppet for these skits if you have a puppet team.

Memory Verse Talk: This is a short talk explaining what the verse means to the children. Memorizing God's Word is important, but it's more important for your students to know what a verse means.

Memory Verse Activity: Children learn by seeing, reading, hearing, and doing. The memory verse activity is a simple tool to help students remember the verse longer.

Game Time: A Game Time slide is included with registration for this curriculum. It isn't necessary to include a game with every week's lesson, but if you do, you should have a fun game that relates to the lessons. Game Time is the place for that. You may also want to save the game for last so, if the adult service runs long, you can play games until the parents arrive to retrieve their children.

Video Clips: *The Journey Countdown* and video clips for some lessons are included with *The Journey* and will be sent in a Zip file through email after you have registered your curriculum. *Building Foundations* doesn't provide video curriculum to teach the lessons. Instead it provides short, fun video clips to help the children remember the lesson in a fun way.

Offering: Lessons include a short talk on why children should give in the offering. You can expand the fun by having an offering contest with the boys against the girls. You can use a scale with buckets or have two offering plates and count the money. Once a month or once a quarter, have a special reward for the winning team.

Praise & Worship: Each week, a time of praise and worship is included to ready the students' hearts to hear the Word of God. This curriculum does not provide music because every church has different musical needs.

Lesson of the Week:

Skit: Two skits about each week's lesson are included. One skit uses a police officer, Officer Shalom, to introduce the memory verse for the day. Another skit uses a silly character named Rhonda the Construction Gal or Ralph the Construction Guy. These skits require few props and only two people, the leader and another worker, making them easy for even small churches to use. The Officer Shalom skits can be used as puppet skits if you have a puppet ministry. The Road/Construction Gal or Guy could also be used with puppets but may need some modification when props are involved.

Bible Story: Each week, a Bible story is included to go with the lesson.

Object Lessons: At least two object lessons illustrate the points of each week's lesson. Resources for the object lessons are not included.

Message: A short message ties up the lesson for the day and asks for a response from the students.

Optional Resources: Optional Resources are included with object lessons and other inactive events as suggestions for additional teaching activities. The props for optional resources are not included but are easy to obtain.

Small Group Chat: Some children's ministries prefer to end each children's service with a small group chat, or they have a small group Bible study at some time during the week. Small group chat questions are included for these purposes. Divide students into small groups of not more than six children. You can divide them by ages or include different ages together. Questions are included to help the leader facilitate a chat with the students about the lesson. Small group sessions will help your students go home with practical applications for what they have learned.

Home Application: Each lesson will include a handout for the children to take home. Each handout will include this week's memory verse, a summary of the lesson, and a Bible reading for each day. This handout is available as a printable PDF download upon registration of this curriculum. This will be helpful guide for parents who have family devotions.

The Journey Part 1: The Road (The Romans Road)

Lesson 1: The Road Out of Eden

Romans 3:23 *For all have sinned and fall short of the glory of God.*

Lesson 2: The Wide Road and the Narrow Road.

Romans 6:23 *For the wages of sin is death, but the gift of God is eternal life in Jesus Christ our Lord.*

Lesson 3: The Road to the Cross

Romans 5:8 *But God demonstrates his own love for us in this: While we were still sinners, Christ died for us.*

Lesson 4: The Road to Damascus

Romans 10:13 *For, "Everyone who calls on the name of the Lord will be saved."*

Lesson 5: The Road to Rome

Romans 10:9 *If you declare with your mouth, "Jesus is Lord," and believe in your heart that God raised him from the dead, you will be saved.*

The Road Lesson 1 - The Road Out of Eden

Focus Point: Everyone has sinned. Everyone needs salvation.

Goal: Children will understand that they can't be good enough to make up for the wrong things they've done. They need to be saved from their sins by asking God to forgive them.

Memory Verse: Romans 3:23 *For all have sinned and fall short of the glory of God.*

Supplies Needed:

- *The Journey* Videos (free with registration)
- *The Journey* Jpeg Slides (free with registration)
- Copies of *The Journey* Family Devotional Sheet (free with registration)
- Road Construction Costume: hardhat, yellow or orange caution vest, walkie-talkie
- police puppet or costume
- piece of paper with a small circle drawn on it
- ball or bean bag
- pieces of paper with memory verse words written on them
- guardrail or barrier
- walkie-talkie or communication device
- Stop sign
- All Have Sinned Object Lesson (optional)

Opening: *The Journey Countdown* or *The Road* or *The Journey* Slide (Available free with registration of this curriculum.)

Welcome: Welcome the children and tell them how happy you are to see them. If you have a smaller church, this is the time how their week has been and ask for prayer requests.

Ask the children about their favorite road trip. Talk about how your so excited because of the next 5 lessons, you and the children will be taking a road trip.

Prayer: Ask a child to pray over the service.

Rules: (use rules slide)

Go over the *5 Ups Rules*: 1. Sit up straight. 2. Listen up. 3. Hush up. 4. Don't get up and run around or go to the bathroom. 5. Worship Up! (stand and participate during praise and worship)

Theme or Activity Songs: Choose one or two fast moving activity songs that goes with the curriculum.

Game Time: Missing the Mark (use game time slide)

Supplies needed: piece of paper with a small circle drawn on it, a ball or bean bag.

Have the children stand 15-20 feet away or farther for the target (the paper with the small circle drawn on it). The idea is to make it impossible to hit the mark.

Let each child take a turn trying to hit the circle with the ball. After each child has a turn, explain that the ball represents good works. The target represents what God expects from us. We can never do enough good works to please God *because* we will always miss the mark.

If you have time, let the children try again, but let them move closer to the target. Then explain that Jesus has provided the way we can hit the mark through His blood.

Memory Verse Skit: Breaking the Law (use *The Road* lesson 1, slide A) This can be used as puppet or live skit.

Supplies needed: police officer puppet or uniform

Peace Officer Shalom: Hi boys and girls. I'm Police Officer Shalom. They call me that because I keep the peace by arresting wrong doers. One day, I stopped somebody going 116 miles per hour in a school zone It's dangerous to go that fast in a school zone. She could have killed a child. I told her to get out of the car because she was under arrest.

The woman told me that she shouldn't be arrested because, even though she had been speeding when I caught her, she'd gone the speed limit most of the day. She thought that because she obeyed the law most of the time, she shouldn't be arrested for the one time she broke the law.

Sometimes people think they can do that with God. They think God should let them into Heaven because most of the time, they do good things. They only do bad things or sin once in a while, so they really aren't sinners.

That's not the way it works. Doing good things doesn't mean you aren't a sinner just like obeying the law most of the time doesn't keep you from being arrested when you break the law. I tried to explain that to the woman I arrested, but she didn't get it.

Romans 3:23 says, "For all have sinned and fall short of the glory of God." Even if they do good things, it doesn't erase their sins. The woman I arrested lost her liscense, had to pay a fine, and do community service for what she did wrong. The judge didn't think she deserved a break for the good things she did either.

Offering: Tell about a time when somebody bought you something because they had done something wrong, how they tried to buy your love or forgiveness with things.

We can never give enough to make up for the wrong things we've done. We give to God because we love Him not to buy His love.

Skit: Guardrails

Supplies needed: Road Guy costume, walkie-talkie, barricade with Do Not Enter sign, can use cones, sawhorses, or chairs for the barricade.

Ralph the Road Guy: (Wanders in carrying a barricade. Whistles as he sets up the barricade to block off the leader.)

Leader: Excuse me. We're having church here. What in the world are you doing?

Ralph: Hi, I'm Ralph the Road Guy. I work on roads to make sure our roadways are safe for travel.

Leader: That doesn't explain what you're doing here. It looks like you're putting up some kind of barrier.

Ralph: That's right, ma'am (or sir). You wouldn't believe the number of drivers who are killed driving off the side of the road. I'm setting up guardrails everywhere I can to make our roadways safe. I want to make sure you don't get hurt on your road trip.

Leader: Well, guardrails are good things, but there's only one problem.

Ralph: What's that?

Leader: This isn't a road. It's a church.

Ralph: (looks around as if he just noticed) I'm so embarrassed. You're right. This is a church not a road.

Leader: That's right, Ralph, but don't feel too bad. Your heart was in the right place. Why don't you tell us a little about guardrails?

Ralph: Guardrails are very important on our nation's roads. They line dangerous places. If someone runs into one, he might do a little damage if his car, but if the guardrail isn't there, he could drive down the side of a mountain or into a river and be killed.

Leader: I agree. Guardrails are important, but not only important to guard roadways. They're also important to guard our lives from sin.

Ralph: (looks confused staring at the guardrail) How can a guardrail protect you from sin?

Leader: Sin is bad. God doesn't want us to sin. And He doesn't want us to inch as close to sin as we possibly can. He wants us to put spiritual guardrails up in our lives so we won't sin.

Ralph: I still don't get it.

Leader: Let me give you an example. Maybe you have a friend who likes to steal. Every time you go to the store with her, she tries to get you to shoplift, to steal something in the store. A guardrail to protect you from being tempted to sin might be to not go to stores with this friend. Tell her you'll go other places with her, but not stores. Going to the store isn't wrong, but not going might be a guardrail that keeps you from doing something wrong.

Ralph: Now, I see what you're saying. Guardrails are not only important on road trips, they're also important in our lives to keep us from sinning.

Leader: That's right, Ralph.

Ralph: (talks in a walkie-talkie) Okay, I'll be right on it. (to leader) I have to go now. There's a pothole on I70 (or chose a highway near you) that needs fixing. Nice meeting you. (Exits)

Memory Verse: Romans 3:23 *For all have sinned and fall short of the glory of God.*

Memory Verse Talk: (use *The Road* lesson 1, slide A)

Have you ever heard someone say he knows he'll go to Heaven because he's a good person? There's a problem with that. Nobody is good enough to go to Heaven because everybody has sinned. Romans 3:23 says "For all have sinned and fall short of the glory of God." That's because God is holy and just. He can't allow sin into to Heaven. But He loves us enough to send His Son, Jesus, to die on the cross. Jesus took the punishment for our sins. We can't be good enough. We can't be holy enough. But we can accept the price Jesus paid. That's how we get to Heaven.

Memory Verse Activity: Word Scramble:

Supplies needed: pieces of paper or index cards.

Place each word of the verse on a separate piece of paper. Make 2 sets. Divide the children into two teams and give them each one set of words. Whoever arranges the set into the memory verse first wins.

Bible Story: Adam and Eve Started It All (Genesis 3)

Supplies needed: table, apple

Assign 4 children to play Adam, Eve, the snake, and an angel. Tell the children to act out the story as you tell it.

Adam and Eve were created by God. They were the very first people on Earth. God gave them a beautiful garden to live in and wonderful fruit to eat. God told them they could eat any fruit they wanted, but there was one fruit they could eat. We don't know what kind of fruit it was, but it could have been an apple. Anyway, God told them they could live with Him in the garden forever as long as they didn't eat the fruit from that one tree.

Everything was going great until one day when the devil disguised as a snake came over to Eve and tried to convince to eat the fruit God told her not to eat. Have Adam stand beside Eve. Have the snake offer the apple to Eve.

Eve could have refused the fruit, but she didn't. She ate some and gave it to her husband, Adam. Have Eve take the apple and pretend to eat it.

Adam could have stopped Eve. He was standing right beside her. He could have refused to eat the fruit too, but he didn't. Adam takes the apple from Eve.

When Adam and Eve disobeyed God and ate the fruit, they sinned against God. Nothing they could do could ever make up for the sin they committed. God told them that they would have to leave the garden forever. Have the angel escort Adam and Eve out of the garden.

God couldn't allow sin to remain with Him, so He had to make Adam and Eve leave, but that's not the end of the story. Because of Adam and Eve, every person is born a sinner. Every one of us has sinned, but God sent His son to take care of that sin. We'll learn more about that later.

Praise and Worship: Choose a couple of fast song and a slow song to lead children into praise and worship. It works well to talk to the children about what worship is and why it's important before you enter into this time. You can have a children's praise team, but until they understand leading praise and worship, have an adult leader or yourself be the worship leader.

Object Lessons:

1. Guardrails

Supplies needed: portion of a guardrail used in the earlier skit or use *The Road* lesson 1, slide B

Some people think that God doesn't want us to sin because He's trying to keep us from having fun, or He want to pounce on us for every little thing, but that's not true. God doesn't want us to sin because He knows the harm it will cause.

First it keeps us away from God and out of Heaven. God is holy. That means He can't have sin in Heaven. He loves us and doesn't want us to sin because He wants us to live forever with Him in Heaven.

Another reason God doesn't want us to sin is because it hurts other people. When you lie or steal or do bad things, other people are affected. God doesn't want your sin to hurt others.

Sin also hurts us. God knows that when we do wrong things, we hurt ourselves. Our lives are changed for the worse whenever we go down the wrong path. Eventually, if we don't make things right, our sin will cause us to live in Hell forever away from God. God doesn't want that for us.

Show guardrail. *This is a guardrail. It's used on dangerous parts of roads to keep people safe. If the guardrails weren't there and we slid off the road, we could go crashing off a mountain or into a river. The guardrails seem like a nuisance, but they keep us from harm. God's Word and laws are guardrails for our lives. They show us where the dangers are and where we need to stay away. Sin will destroy us. God's guardrails keep us safe.*

2. Everyone Has Sinned

Supplies needed: Stop Sign or use *The Road* lesson 1, slide C

Have any of you ever heard someone say that people are really good at heart? When they say that, they're saying that nobody really is bad inside, but the Bible says that sin is bad. God doesn't want anyone to sin. He's given His Word, the Bible, as a Stop Sign to show us what sin is and to keep us from sinning, but every one of us has ignored that sign. The Bible says we've all sinned. I've sinned, and every leader and student in this room has sinned.

I'm going to ask you some questions, and I want you to raise your hands if these apply to you. Make sure to raise your hand when appropriate to show the children that you've sinned.

- *Have any of you ever disobeyed your parents?*

The Journey: The Road, Lesson 1

- *Have any of you ever lied?*
- *Have you ever cheated in a game with your friends? That's lying.*
- *Have you ever thought bad things about somebody?*
- *Have you ever stolen anything?*
- *Have you ever been jealous of someone?*
- *Have you ever been mean to someone?*

All of those things are sins, and we're all guilty of sinning. Every one of us deserves to be punished for our sin. That's why Jesus died on the cross. He took the punishment for our sin. But we need to be willing to confess our sin and ask Jesus to forgive. We need to accept what Jesus has done to take our punishment for our sin.

Optional Object Lesson: Jesus, You, and Sin

This YouTube video has instructions for an object lesson, or you can show the video. https://youtu.be/8Z_SMrnEiaI

Message: What to Do About Sin

Have the children close their eyes, and instruct them to ask God to show them any sins they've done that they haven't made right. After a few moments, have them open their eyes and look at you. As you mention each step, lead the children in a short prayer.

These are the steps you want to take when God shows you that you've sinned.

- *Confess your sin. Admit you're a sinner and that you've sinned against God.*
- *Remember that God took the punishment for your sin when Jesus died on the cross. If you haven't asked Jesus into your heart, ask him to be your Savoir.*
- *Ask God to forgive you of your sin.*
- *Ask God to help you not do that sin again. Tell Him you want to live for him instead of sinning against Him.*
- *Thank God for forgiving you.*
- *If you've sinned against another person (being mean to someone, disobeying parents, lying), as soon as you can, go to that person, confess your sin, and ask them to forgive you.*

For response time, lead the children in a prayer, have each child find a quiet place to pray, or have an altar call and pray for the children who come forward.

Small Group Chat:

Ask these question as discussion starters.

Talk about how when Adam and Eve sinned, they had to take a road trip out of Eden. *Have you ever taken a road trip you didn't like?*

What do you think a judge would say if you broke the law and explained to him that most of the time you obey the law?

How is that different than people who try to be good enough without getting saved?

What should you do if you sin against someone?

The Journey: The Road, Lesson 2

The Road Lesson 2 – The Wide Road and the Narrow Road

Focus Point: Sin – the wide road – leads to death. Salvation in Jesus Christ – the wide road – leads to eternal life.

Goal: Children will learn that everyone has to make a choice between accepting Jesus Christ as their Savior or staying in their sins. Most people will choose to stay in their sins and face eternal death.

Memory Verse Status: Romans 6:23 *For the wages of sin is death, but the gift of God is eternal life in Christ Jesus our Lord.*

Supplies Needed:

- *The Journey* Videos (free with registration)
- *The Journey* Jpeg Slides (free with registration)
- Copies of *The Journey* Family Devotional Sheet (free with registration)
- Road Construction Costume: hardhat, yellow or orange caution vest, walkie-talkie
- police puppet or costume
- chalkboard or marker board with chalk or dry erase markers
- a crown (If you have a Burger King near you, they will give you a crown for free or you can make it out of construction paper)
- 3 boxes with A, B, and C written on them
- 2 really good prizes and 1 not so good prize
- 3 candy bars
- Road Closed and Dead End sign made by printing *The Journey* jpeg image with a color printer and gluing it onto cardboard
- Narrow Path and Wide Path signs made by printing *The Journey* jpeg image with a color printer and gluing in onto cardboard

Opening: *The Journey Countdown* or *The Road* or *The Journey* Intro Slide (Available free with registration of this curriculum.)

Welcome: Your students had a number of choices about how to spend today. They could have slept in, or played video games, or watched TV. They might have decided to play at a sports game or spend the night at a friend's house, but they decided to come to church. If someone made the decision for you like your parents, they made the right choice.

We all have choices to make, but when we decide between God and something else, God is always the right choice.

Prayer: Ask a child to pray over the service.

Rules: (use rules slide)

Go over the *5 Ups Rules*: 1. Sit up straight. 2. Listen up. 3. Hush up. 4. Don't get up and run around or go to the bathroom. 5. Worship Up! (stand and participate during praise and worship)

Theme or Activity Songs: Choose one or two fast moving activity songs that goes with the curriculum.

Memory Verse Skit: (use *The Road* lesson 1, slide A) This can be used as puppet or live skit.

Supplies needed: police officer puppet or uniform

Officer Shalom: Hi boys and girls. In my line of work, I see a lot of people who have messed up their lives by making bad choices. Some of them started out all right, but then they decided to follow the wrong crowd or do what would make them look cool with their friends. They didn't start out deciding they wanted to be a criminal or a drug addict. Some of them wanted to be doctors, or firefighters, or baseball players. Some of them even wanted to become police officers, but they kept choosing to go down the wrong road. They ended up where they didn't want to be. Today's memory verse talks about the choice each of us has to make. Romans 6:23 "For the wages of sin is death, but the gift of God is eternal life in Christ Jesus our Lord." Make the right choice.

Game Time: Choose Wisely (use game time slide)

Supplies needed: 3 boxes with A, B, and C written on them. 2 really good prizes and 1 not so good prize, 3 candy bars

Preparation: Place one item in each box so it can't be seen by the children. Choose 3 children to play this game. If you want to play again, you'll need 3 more prizes and boxes.

When I was young, there was a game show on TV called "Let's Make A Deal". If you got a correct answer, you won a prize, but the catch was you would have to choose the prize you wanted without seeing it first. Let's try it.

Ask these questions about last week's lesson. The first three children to get the questions right get to play the game.

Where did Adam and Eve live before they sinned?

Who tempted Eve to eat the fruit?

How many people in the world have sinned?

As the children answer questions correctly, have them choose box A, B, or C. After they choose, tell them they can have the prize in that box, or they can have the candy bar you're holding.

Talk to the children about how they had to choose which prize they wanted.

We all have to make choices in life. Some choices are unimportant like what color shirt we want to wear. Other choices can affect our whole lives. Whatever choices we make, we have to live with the consequences. The choice we're talking about today not only affects our life on Earth. It determines where we'll spend eternity. We need to choose wisely.

Offering: *The Bible says that each of us should determine how much we want to give in the offering. Once we've decided how much we want to give, we should give it cheerfully because God loves a cheerful giver. Let's give cheerfully today by clapping and cheering before the offering.*

Memory Verse: Romans 6:23 *For the wages of sin is death, but the gift of God is eternal life in Christ Jesus our Lord.*

Memory Verse Talk: (use *The Road* lesson 2, slide A)

We learned last week that everyone has sinned. Today's verse tells us that when we sin, we earn death, but we don't have to receive the punishment we deserve. When Jesus died on the cross, He took the punishment our sin deserves. All we have to do is accept His sacrifice as a free gift. It's our choice. We can accept the punishment we deserve or we can accept the free gift God gave us, life forever in Jesus Christ. Romans 6:23 says "For the wages of sin is death, but the gift of God is eternal life in Christ Jesus our Lord."

Memory Verse Activity: Verse Relay

Supplies needed: chalkboard or marker board and chalk or dry erase markers

Divide the children into two or more teams. Have the teams form lines across from a chalk or white board. Place a good piece of chalk and eraser at the board in front of each team. On a cue, have the first child of each team run to the board and write the first word of the verse, then run back to the line. The next child of the team will write the next word and so on. See which team can finish first. Allow all teams to finish before playing again. If some of your children are not readers, you can team them up with older children.

Skit: Which Road Should I Take?

Supplies needed: Road Guy costume, walkie-talkie, Do Not Enter Sign – you can make this by printing jpeg image *The Road* Lesson 2, Slide B with a color printer and gluing in on cardboard

Ralph the Road Guy: (Wanders in carrying a "Do Not Enter" sign and places it in front of the stage.)

Leader: Ralph, what's this sign? What are you up to now?

Ralph: You know I'm a road guy.

Leader: So?

Ralph: Today, I'm blocking off roads that are closed so cars can't get onto them. See, I have this "Do Not Enter" sign.

Leader: I can understand that. It's dangerous for cars to go on roads that are closed. There might be a bridge that is out, or construction workers might be digging holes that cars can fall into. Worse yet, a car might hit a construction worker working on the road.

Ralph: That's right. Sometimes roads are even closed because of landslides, flooding, and other natural disasters. These road sign warn motorists to stay away.

Leader: Tell me, Ralph. Do you ever have motorists drive around the "Do Not Enter" sign?

Ralph: All the time. Then we have to go get them when they run into trouble. We have detour sign whenever we close a road to show drivers which road is safe, but sometimes they don't listen.

Leader: That's the way it is in the Bible too.

Ralph: I don't get it. The Bible talks about closed roads?

Leader: In a way. The Bible talks about the narrow road that leads to eternal life, but it also talks about the wide road that leads to destruction. Even so, most people will decide to take the wide road.

Ralph: You mean there are roads in the Bible. I didn't know there were cars back then.

Leader: It's is not the same kind of road. The Bible talks about paths we can take in our lives. We can continue to sin against God and not accept that He is the only way to salvation. If we do that, our lives are on the wide path. We ask Jesus to forgive us for our sin and follow after Him, then our lives will be on the narrow path.

Ralph: Sounds like the wide path needs a big "Do Not Enter" sign.

Leader: In a way, that's what the Bible is. It tells us which path to take.

Ralph: I sure want to take that path. (talks in walkie-talkie) Yeah, I'll get right on it. (turns to leader) I need to post some more of these signs.

Leader: Before you go, Ralph, I have a question. Why did you put a "Do Not Enter" sign here?

Ralph: A while back, I heard you tell the children not to come in the stage area. I figured you could use a sign to remind them.

Leader: Good thinking, Ralph. Bye.

Object Lessons:

1. The Wide Path and the Narrow Path

Supplies needed: narrow path and wide path signs made out of cardboard or written on construction paper

In the Bible, the wide path represents people who have rejected Jesus as their savior and who are living in sin. The narrow path represents people who have accepted Jesus as their savior and are living a life that pleases Him. I'm going to make some statements, and I want you to tell me if someone making this statement is on the wide path or the narrow path. After you shout out your answers, I'll hold up the sign that tells which it is.

Chose some of the following or come up with some of your own:

- *I want to watch TV shows where there is a lot of cussing.* (Wide Path)
- *I like to read the Bible.* (Narrow Path)
- *I don't like to talk to some of the kids in school because my friends don't like them.* (Wide

Path)
- *I clean my room when my mother tells me too.* (Narrow Path)
- *I go to church only when there isn't something better happening.* (Wide Path)
- *I give the first 10% of my allowance to God.* (Narrow Path)
- *I love to worship God.* (Narrow Path)
- *It doesn't matter whether you believe in Jesus or not if you are a good person.* (Wide Path)
- *A little lie occasionally doesn't hurt anyone.* (Wide Path)
- *I sometimes play video games or read books that have occult in them.* You may have to explain what the occult is. (Wide Path)
- *I've asked Jesus to forgive me of my sins.* (Narrow Path)

2. Road Closed

Supplies needed: Road Closed road sign and Do Not Enter sign or use *The Road* lesson 2 slide B & C

Sometimes drivers don't follow road signs. When they don't, it can cause a lot of problems.

Show Do Not Enter sign or use *The Road* lesson 2 jpeg. *Here we have a Do Not Enter sign. Many times, this sign is posted because there are dangerous conditions ahead. A bridge may be out, or the road might be blocked by a tree or torn up by a storm. Road Maintenance workers don't put up these signs for fun. They do it because there is a reason to close the road. What do you think would happen if a driver saw one of these signs and decided to go ahead anyone because the road looks good?*

Allow children to answer. Offer suggestions of some bad things that could happen.

(show Road Closed sign or use *The Road* lesson 2 jpeg) *The Road Closed sign warns drivers that even though the road may look good, there's danger ahead. God has a road closed sign too. Most people take the wide path of doing whatever they want because it looks good and everyone else is on that path. But God's Word tells us that God has placed a big Road Closed Sign on that path. If you decide to take that road anyway, it leads to death. God wants us to take the narrow road because that leads to life.*

Praise and Worship: Choose a couple of fast song and a slow song to lead children into praise and worship. It works well to talk to the children about what worship is and why it's important before you enter into this time. You can have a children's praise team, but until they understand leading praise and worship, have an adult leader or yourself be the worship leader.

Video: Narrow Road (*The Road* videos available upon registration of materials)

Bible Story: Two Kings (1 Samuel)

Supplies Needed: 1 crown (If you have a Burger King near you, they will give you a crown for free or you can make it out of construction paper)

Tell the children that to your right is the narrow road and to your left is the wide road. Chose two children to be kings and place the crown on one of their heads. Have that child represent Saul.

The Bible talks about two kings of Israel who made very different choices about the path they would follow.

The first king's name was Saul. When he became king, the people loved him because he helped them by defeating their enemies. God was with him, but after a while, he started loving the praises of the people. He would do things he knew God wasn't pleased with because it would make the people happy.

One day, the prophet of God told him to go to war with another country but to destroy all of the property of that nation. The king and the people weren't allowed to keep anything. Saul was afraid the people wouldn't like him if he didn't let them keep some of the stuff they found, plus he wanted some of the sheep and goats, so he disobeyed God and took them.

God told the prophet Samuel that He was very unhappy with Saul and that He would remove the kingdom for Saul. Samuel went to Saul to tell him this, but before he was able, Saul came to him and announced that he had obeyed God. Samuel asked Saul where the bleating of the sheep he heard was coming from. Saul lied, then excused what he did by saying he was afraid of the people. Which side do you think Saul belongs on – the narrow path to my right or the wide path to my left?

Have the child representing Saul move to the left and place the crown of the child's head who represents David.

God told Samuel to anoint another man as king, David. God said David would be a man after his own heart. David had to wait to be king, but he was faithful to God while he waited. When he was made king, he did what God told him to do, but one day, he did something wrong. He tried to hide it, but God sent the prophet Nathan to tell David that God knew what he did.

David didn't make excuses. He confessed his sin, repented, and asked God to forgive. God did forgive him, and he continued to be a great king who followed God. Which side do you think David belongs on – the narrow path to my left or the wide path to my right?

Have the child representing David go to your right.

When you decide to follow God, that doesn't mean you won't sometimes fail, but if you confess you sins and get on the right path again, God will lead you and guide you. Sometimes the path is hard, but it's worth it.

Message: Your Choice

There are two groups of children here today. One group is following Jesus on the narrow path that leads to life everlasting. The other group is on the wide path. Some of you are on the wide path have never asked Jesus into your heart to be your Lord and Savior. All you have to do to get on the right path is to ask Him to forgive you and come into your heart.

Others of you started out on right path, like King Saul, but you haven't been obeying God's Word and commands. You've left the narrow path and got on the wide path. Maybe you've been doing sins God doesn't want you to do like lying or disobeying your parents, or you might have started putting other things before God. Whatever it is, you can be like King David and get back on the right path by asking God to forgive you and to help you.

For response time, lead the children in a prayer or have an altar call and pray for the children who come forward.

Small Group Chat:

Ask this question as a discussion starter.

What things are you giving up to be a Christ follower?

Is there anything worth not giving up to follow Jesus?

Talk to the children about how Jesus is worth much more than anything they give up.

The Journey: The Road, Lesson 2

The Road Lesson 3 - The Road to the Cross

Focus Point: God loves us. That is why Jesus died for us.

Goal: Children will learn that Jesus died on the cross for our sins because God has always loved us, even before we were saved.

Memory Verse: Romans 5:8 *But God demonstrates his own love for us in this: While we were still sinners, Christ died for us.*

Supplies Needed:

- *The Journey* Videos (free with registration)
- *The Journey* Jpeg Slides (free with registration)
- Copies of *The Journey* Family Devotional Sheet (free with registration)
- Road Construction Costume: hardhat, yellow or orange caution vest, walkie-talkie
- police puppet or costume
- One Way sign made this by printing jpeg image with a color printer and gluing in on cardboard
- a heart shaped mushy card
- a photo of a family member
- friendship bracelet
- slide of Christ dying on the cross
- play money
- brownie
- stained shirt
- sign that says "God is Love"
- a marker board with the word SIN written in big letters and an eraser
- 2 glasses and red food coloring (optional)
- one dollar bill

Opening: *The Journey Countdown* or *The Road* or *The Journey* Slide (Available free with registration of this curriculum.)

Welcome: Welcome the children and tell them how happy you are to see them. If you have a smaller church, this is the time how their week has been and ask for prayer requests.

Ask *have you ever been in love*? Give the children a chance to respond. *Sometimes we have a mistaken notion of what love really is. We think it's gooey, mushy feelings about someone we really like. But that's not real love, and that's not the great love Jesus Christ showed when he died on the cross for us. Today we're going to learn about that kind of great love.*

Prayer: Ask a child to pray over the service.

Rules: (use rules slide)

Go over the *5 Ups Rules*: 1. Sit up straight. 2. Listen up. 3. Hush up. 4. Don't get up and run around or go to the bathroom. 5. Worship Up! (stand and participate during praise and worship)

Theme or Activity Songs: Choose one or two fast moving activity songs that goes with the curriculum.

Memory Verse Skit: (*The Road* lesson 3, slide A)

Supplies needed: Police officer puppet or person dressed as a police officer

Officer Shalom: Hello, boys and girls. Once while I was on duty, I saw a great act of love. A criminal wanted to abduct a girl about your age. A teenage boy stepped in front of the child and wouldn't let the man near her. The bad man pulled out a gun and told the teenager to move or he would shoot him. I made it to the scene right about then.

The teenager told the man he would have to go through him to get to the girl. I didn't have a clear shot at the man with the gun. I ordered him to put down his weapon and rushed toward him.

That's when I heard the gun fire. He'd shot the teenager. At that point, I managed to get the situation under control. I tackled the man with the gun and arrested him. Then I called for backup and an ambulance.

After I locked the man in the back of my squad car, I sat beside the boy and held his hand. The little girl cried and asked if he was going to be all right. I didn't know, but I told her she should pray for him.

As I sat there, I got to thinking. If it hadn't been for the teenager who was willing to give his life for a girl he didn't know, the man would have snatched her before we got there. That teenager saved the girl's life.

This story has a happy ending. After surgery, the teenager was fine and even received a medal for bravery from the mayor.

Jesus loves us like that teenager loved that girl in trouble. He died on the cross for us. Today's memory verse, Romans 5:8, says "But God demonstrates his own love for us in this: While we were still sinners, Christ died for us." I'm glad God loves us enough to die for us.

Game Time: What Do I Love? (use game time slide)

We use the word love in a lot of different ways. Sometimes we say things like "I love pizza" or "I love my new video game." That isn't really love. Jesus showed his love when He died for us.

This game is based on the game I Spy.

Explain the rules of the game. The child who is in front will think of an object he or she "loves" and will give the first letter of the object. Give each child a chance to ask a question or call on children whose hands are raised. When it is a child's turn, he or she will ask a question about what the child up front loves. The child in the front must answer honestly. If a child thinks he knows what the answer is, he can ask "Is it a ?." If he's right, he gets to be it.

Skit: Ralph the Road Guy – One Way

Supplies needed: Road Guy costume, walkie-talkie, One Way Sign – you can make this by printing jpeg image *The Road* Lesson 3, Slide B with a color printer and gluing in on cardboard or making a One Way Sign out of cardboard.

Ralph the Road Guy: Hi everyone. Do you know what this is? (holds up One Way Sign)

Leader: Of course we know what it is. It's a One Way road sign.

Ralph: Today the boss told me to put them all over town.

Leader: It's dangerous to go the wrong way on a one-way street. You're doing a good work out there by warning people.

Ralph: Yeah, I guess, but I had this brilliant idea.

Leader: Uh, oh. Sometimes your ideas don't work very well.

Ralph: Like what?

Leader: Remember the time you thought the road crew should make a funeral lane so the other cars didn't have to slow down or stop for funeral processions.

Ralph: I still think that's a good idea. I can't figure out why the boss didn't like it.

Leader: Anyway, let's hear your new idea.

Ralph: I'm going to keep one of the signs to hang on the side of my car.

Leader: Why would you want to do that?

Ralph: Think about it a minute. If I have a one-way sign pointing the direction I'm going, I'll never have to worry about one-way streets. I'll always be going the right way on them because my sign will be pointed the right way.

Leader: Ralph, that's a terrible idea. You can't do that.

Ralph: Yes, I can, if I keep one of the signs for myself.

Leader: Why do you hang those signs on roads?

Ralph: To keep people from going the wrong way on one-way streets.

Leader: That's right. Those signs protect people from accidents. If you go the wrong way on a one-way street, you might hit somebody's car because they're going the opposite direction. You wouldn't want to do that.

Ralph: I won't be going the wrong way because I'll have my sign.

Leader: But the other drivers will see the sign on the side of the road and will be headed the other way.

Ralph: So, they can follow the sign they want, and I'll follow the sign I want.

Leader: Ralph, that's not the way it works. You remind me of some people who think it doesn't matter what religion you follow as long as you're a good person.

Ralph: What's wrong with that?

Leader: The Bible teaches us that no one is good. Everyone has sinned, but our loving God provided a way of escape by sending Jesus to die on the cross. We need to accept His free gift of salvation because it's the only way to get right with God. All other ways lead to hell.

Ralph: You mean God tells me there's only one way to be saved is because He loves us and doesn't want us to go the wrong way.

Leader: That's right, Ralph.

Ralph: Maybe I'll hold off on my sign idea until I think it through.

Leader: I think that would be best. You should consider taking the only way of salvation too by accepting God's free gift.

Ralph: (talks in walkie-talkie) I plan to put the signs up now, boss. I'll get on it right away. (turns to leader) I have to go now, but I'll think about what you said.

Offering: *Jesus gave His life for us because of his great love for us. One way we can show we love Him is by giving a tenth of our money to God. That means if you get a dollar for allowance, you decide to give 10 cents in the offering. That is called tithe.*

Memory Verse: Romans 5:8 *But God demonstrates his own love for us in this: While we were still sinners, Christ died for us.*

Memory Verse Talk: (use *The Road* lesson 3, slide A)

This verse talks about God's great love for us. He died for us when we were still sinners. When we sin, it hurts God. How many of you would still love someone who treated you bad and hurt you all the time? That would be hard, wouldn't it? That's the kind of great love God has for us.

Memory Verse Activity: Quote the Verse If...

Chose different groups to quote the memory verse with you. For instance: Quote the memory verse if you (have blue on, have brown eyes, ate breakfast this morning, like to play basketball, etc.)

Object Lessons:

1. Object Lesson: Different Kinds of Love (use *The Road* Lesson 3, Slide C)

Supplies Needed: A DVD or picture of a movie you love, a heart shaped mushy card, a photo of a family member, friendship bracelet, slide C of Christ dying on the cross

We've already talked about how there are different kinds of love. That's important because when the Bible talks about Christ's love for us, we need to know what that means.

First, there's love we have for things. Show the movie. *For instance, I love this movie.* Talk about the movie and why you love it so much. *Is that the kind of love Christ had when He died on the cross for us? I wouldn't die for this movie.*

The next kind of love is eros love. Show the card. *That's the kind of love that is all mushy. Your parents have this kind of love when they kiss and hug each other. Some of you may have had this kind of love for a classmate. This isn't the kind of love Christ had. When people have this kind of emotional love and it never grows into another kind of love, they end up with broken hearts. Mushy feelings come and go, but Christ's love last forever.*

The next kind of love is called storge love. Show a photo of a family member. *This is getting closer because I would die for my family, but it still isn't the same kind of love because sometimes family members hurt us badly enough that we can't spend time with them anymore. Sometimes families don't get along.*

Then there's philia love. Show friendship bracelet. *That's the love we have for our friends. Christ has that love for us. That's why he calls us His friends. But Christ's love even goes further than that. We love our friends when they're good to us, but if a friend betrays us or is mean to us all of the time, we stop being friends. We lose the philia kind of love we have for them.*

Christ loves us with agape love. He hates sin. When we sin, it's like we are hurting and betraying Christ, but that doesn't stop His love for us. Show slide C of Christ dying on the cross. *Christ loves us so much that He took the punishment for our sin while we were still sinners by dying on the cross for us. His love for us knows no bounds no matter how much we betray Him by sinning against Him. Christ's agape love for us is unconditional. That means no matter what we do, He still loves us.*

2. One Way to Salvation with Optional Object lesson Ending

Supplies needed: One Way sign or *The Road* lesson 3, slide B, play money, brownie, stained shirt, sign that says "God is Love". You will also need a marker board or chalkboard with the word SIN written in big letters and an eraser.

Optional Supplies: Gospel Illusion dissolve paper (you can buy this online or at a magic shop), 2 clear glasses – one filled with water, red food coloring at the bottom of the other glass.

Preparation: Have children come forward and hold the following. 1st child – one way sign, 2nd child – play money, 3rd child – brownie on a paper plate (warn the child not to touch the brownie), 4th child – stained shirt, 5th child – sign that says God is Love.

Have first child step forward.

Some people think there's more than one way to Heaven. But Jesus said, "I am the way the truth and the life. No man comes to the father but by me." That's because of what we learned the last couple of weeks. Everyone has sinned, and everyone has to choose to take the right path, to be saved.

Show play money.

Some people think if they give enough money or time to the church, they'll make it to Heaven. But there isn't enough money in the world to erase even one sin. That would be like someone who murdered someone else saying they shouldn't go to jail because they'll pay the court and victim's family money. Money doesn't erase what they did.

Have third child step forward.

Some people think that even though they've done wrong things, they've done more good than bad so God will let them into Heaven. This brownie is made with a lot of good ingredients. But I also put some rat poison in it. There are more good ingredients than rat poison. Do the good ingredients make the poison go away? Good deeds don't make our sins go away either.

Have the fourth child step forward.

Others think that it doesn't matter what you believe, there are many ways to take care of sin and many ways to God. This shirt is stained beyond fixing. Tell the students how the shirt was stained and all the different things you used to try to get the stain out. *It doesn't matter what product I use, the stain won't come out. There are different ways to get stained out, but once a shirt is stained this bad, none of them will work. This shirt is like sin.*

Have the fifth child step forward.

We just learned during the last object lesson that God loves us so much that Christ died on the cross for our sins. Some people think that because God is love, He'll let us go to Heaven. We don't have to accept Him as our Lord and Savior. The problem with that is that although God is love, He is also holy and just. He can't allow sin to go unpunished. That's why He sent Jesus to die on the cross. Jesus took the punishment for our sin because He loves us, but He won't force us to accept Him and His free gift. When He reveals Himself to us, we can refuse the only way to salvation, through Him, but that means we will be punished for our sin after we die.

Option 1 Ending: marker board and eraser

Erase the word sin.

There is only one way to erase the sin in our lives and be saved. We have to confess that we've sinned, accept Jesus died for our sin, and ask Him to become our Lord. There is only one way to salvation.

Option 2 Ending (Optional): 2 glasses, red food coloring, dissolvo paper from *The Journey Additional Resources*

Preparation: Before service, fill one glass with water. Put 2 to 3 drops of food coloring in the bottom of the second glass.

Hold up the dissolvo paper. *I want a very brave volunteer.* Pick an older child or a worker. Say to the volunteer, *write on this paper the worst sin you've ever committed. Don't worry. Nobody's going to look at it.* While the volunteer is writing, tease him by saying things like *Having trouble thinking of just one? Only one sin. We haven't got all day.*

Fold the paper in two and place it in the second glass. Hold the glasses up making sure to cover the food coloring with your hand. Pour the water into the second glass. Then pour it back and forth a few times. Tell the volunteer to dish the paper out of the water. Of course it's gone. Talk about who when we accept Jesus as our savior, He removes our sin as far as the east is from the west, as if it never happened.

Praise and Worship

Bible Story: Jesus Died on the Cross (John 19:1-30)

Supplies Needed: YouTube video clip or whip, crown of thorns, nails, mallet, wooden cross or beam. Instrumental music.

This is a very sobering story. There are three ways to do this story. You can use the objects listed as you play instrumental music low in the background while you tell this story. Or you can find a YouTube Video that shows the crucifixion of Jesus Christ with instrumental music playing and show the video while you're telling the story. The ages of your students may affect your decision or what YouTube Video you decide to use. The ages of your children may also affect how detailed you are in the descriptions.

When God created the human race, He wanted us to have a relationship with Him. He created all the animals, but they have no choice but to do what He wants. God gives us a choice to decide if we want to live for God or against God, but even though He's a good God who loves us, the first man and woman decided to sin.

God was sad that man decided to sin because He is also Holy and Just. He can't allow sin into Heaven. Even though we've all sinned, God still loves us, so He had a plan of redemption before the world was created to bring us back to Him.

God loves us so much that He came to Earth as a baby named Jesus, grew up like all of you are doing, and lived a life without sin. He did that to show us the way to live to be close to Him, but that's not the only reason He became a man.

God knows the punishment for sin is death, so Jesus loves us so much He was willing to die on the cross for our sins so that we could live forever with God.

Show the whip. *Jesus was beaten with a whip like this one. It had nine straps and each strap had bones, hooks and rocks tied one the end.*

Show the crown of thorns. *After Jesus was whipped 39 times, they dug a crown of sharp thorns into his head.*

Show the mallet and nails. *They made Jesus carry his cross to the top of a hill. Then they made him lay on the cross. They hammered nails into his hands and feet. Some people think they hammered the nails into His wrists because the weight of the body would have torn through His hands. Others think they tied Him to the cross and hammered His hands. Imagine the pain He went through to be punished for our sins.*

Show the cross. *Jesus died on a cross like this to pay for our sins. When He was nailed on the cross and lifted up, He couldn't breathe without lifting His body using the hands and feet with nails in them and then falling back down. People who were crucified normally died when they were too tired to lift themselves up. Jesus died after He said, "It is finished." The price for our sins was paid. Then He was buried and on the third day rose again to show our sins had been forgiven and He is the Lord of all.*

Message:

Supplies needed: one dollar bill, play money dollar bill

How many of you would like this crisp new dollar bill? Give children a chance to respond. *Okay, I'll give this to anyone who wants it bad enough to come up and get it first.* Some children will catch on and run up to grab the dollar. Others will sit back not sure if they should.

Suppose I offered you that dollar bill and nobody would take it. Choose the child who took the dollar bill or another child to help you and have the child act out the motions. Show the play money. *Let's pretend that I gave you this dollar and it was real like the other one. What if I couldn't get you to accept the dollar bill?* Have the child cross his arms and refuse to take it.

But it's free. I'm giving it to you. It will buy a candy bar or a small toy. You can use it for anything you want. Have the child take the play money, tear it to pieces, stomp on it, and throw it away.

Even though Jesus died for our sins, God still gives us a choice. We can choose to accept what He has done for us and give our lives to Him like He gave His life for us, or we can decide to live our own way and tell God we don't care how much He loves us. We don't want to accept His free gift of salvation. When we do that, it's as if we're stomping on His sacrifice and throwing his gift of salvation away. The choice is yours.

This would be a good time for an altar call. First ask children forward for prayer who want to accept Jesus' sacrifice for them. Then call us the children who want to pray and thank God for what He has done for them. You may lead them in a time of worship to praise God for His gift of salvation.

Small Group Chat:

Ask these question as discussion starters.

How did Jesus show His love for us?

After what Jesus did for us, how can we show Him we love Him?

What about people who don't love Jesus? How can we show His love to them?

Jesus died for us while we were still sinners. Should we love others who don't know Him? Should we love others who treat us bad?

The Road Lesson 4: The Road to Damascus

Focus Point: Anyone can be saved.

Goal: Children will learn how they can be saved.

Memory Verse Status: Romans 10:13 *Everyone who calls on the name of the Lord will be saved.*

Supplies Needed:

- *The Journey* Videos (free with registration)
- *The Journey* Jpeg Slides (free with registration)
- Copies of *The Journey* Family Devotional Sheet (free with registration)
- Road Construction Costume: hardhat, yellow or orange caution vest, walkie-talkie
- police puppet or costume
- Go sign made by printing jpeg image in color and gluing it on cardboard
- Stop sign made by printing jpeg image in color and gluing it on cardboard
- Yield sign made by printing jpeg image in color and gluing it on cardboard
- U-Turn sign made by printing jpeg image in color and gluing it on cardboard
- toy or real frog

Opening: *The Journey Countdown* or *The Road* or *The Journey* Slide (Available free with registration of this curriculum.)

Welcome: Welcome the children and tell them how happy you are to see them. If you have a smaller church, this is the time how their week has been and ask for prayer requests.

Review the last three weeks.

Have you ever done something that you wished you had a chance to do differently. The apostle Paul felt that way too. He'd done some horrible things in his life, but he learned that no matter what we've done, we can make a U-turn and change our lives for the better.

Prayer: Ask a child to pray over the service.

Rules: (use rules slide)

Go over the *5 Ups Rules*: 1. Sit up straight. 2. Listen up. 3. Hush up. 4. Don't get up and run around or go to the bathroom. 5. Worship Up! (stand and participate during praise and worship)

Theme or Activity Songs: Choose one or two fast moving activity songs that goes with the curriculum.

Memory Verse Skit: (use *The Road* lesson 4, slide A)

Supplies needed: Police officer puppet or person dressed as a police officer

Officer Shalom: Hello, boys and girls. Nobody wants the police around when they're committing crimes or doing something wrong. That's because they know the police will come and arrest them. But if you're not a criminal, there's no need to fear the police. Police officers are in law enforcement because they want to help people. Whenever someone calls 911 and says that they are in danger, the person on the other end of the line always sends the help these people need.

That's where I come in. If I'm sent to someone's house, it's usually because someone is trying to hurt the person who called in some way or they've been in an accident. They need help. That's why they've called 911. Because they've called, I'm there to help them. It's the same with God. Whenever we call out to Him, He's there to help us. Only when we call God, we don't have to be afraid of Him even if we have done something wrong because He wants to save us no matter what we've done.

Romans 10:13 says *"The Scripture says, "Anyone who asks the Lord for help will be saved."* I'm glad God loves us enough to answer our call for help. Stay safe out there.

Game Time: Calling For Help Relay (use game time slide)

Supplies needed: sash or piece of rope

This game is based on a relay race. Divide the children into two teams at the back of the room. The first child on each team runs to the front of the room yelling "help, help." The second person must wait until the first person touches the front wall, step, stage, etc., then he runs to the front to save the first person. He does that by grabbing the person's hand, (you can also have them both hold on to a piece or rope of a sash) then they both run to the back and tap the next person in line. The next person does the same as the first person.

If there aren't an even number of students on each side, you may want to assign one or two people on each team to be the ones who need help each time.

Skit: Ralph the Road Guy – U-Turns

Supplies needed: Road Guy Costume, walkie-talkie, U-Turn Sign – you can make this by printing jpeg image from *The Road* lesson 4, slide B with a color printer and gluing in on cardboard.

Leader: Hello, Ralph. What did your boss think of you hanging a one way sign on your car last week?

Ralph: He was pretty mad about it. He said that if I try a stunt like that, I'll be fired. Now he has me hanging these signs. (shows no U-turn signs) I guess the cops are getting pretty frustrated with all the people in the city making U-turns.

Leader: Ralph, why don't you explain to the children what a U-Turn is?

Ralph: Sure. A U-turn is a 180-degree turn made by a vehicle on the road.

Leader: What does that mean?

The Journey: The Road, Lesson 4

Ralph: Say you're driving down the road and you miss the parking lot of Chick-fil-A. (or another restaurant the kids know about) I love Chick-fil-A. (have Ralph go on about his favorite meal at the restaurant) You have a few choices. First, you can turn into another parking lot and then pull around and go the other way.

Leader: That's hard to do if it's a busy street. I've tried that and was stuck in traffic for a long time.

Ralph: Some store owners don't like to have you pull in their parking lots to turn around either. So that's not always the best option. Second, you can go around the block, but that doesn't always work either. The next street up might be a one-way street going the wrong way, or it might be a few miles up the road.

Leader: I can see how that would be a problem.

Ralph: That leaves the third option. You can do a U-turn which means you turn your car around in a U shape and start going the other way.

Leader: That sounds like the easiest option.

Ralph: It may be the easiest, but in some areas, it can be dangerous. In some cities and states, U turns are even illegal. When a U turn is illegal in a state or city where it's normally legal, these signs let the driver know not to make a U-turn. That's why I'm hanging up these signs.

Leader: That makes sense. I sure am happy that when we call out to God, He allows U-turns.

Ralph: What do you mean by that? I'm shocked that God wants you to break the law and make U-turns even where they're illegal. That's dangerous.

Leader: No, not in a car. God allows U-turns in our lives. When we're going in the wrong direction and doing wrong things, all we have to do is call on the Lord, and He'll help us make a U-turn and follow Him.

Ralph: There are some things I've done in my life where I wish I could make some U-turns.

Leader: All you have to do is call on the Lord, and He'll help you get saved and turn your life around.

Ralph: I think on that some more. (talks in walkie talkie) Yes, sir. I'll get those signs down to Broad Street right away. (turns to leader) Thanks for telling me about God's U-turns. I have to go now.

Offering: This might be a good time to take an offering for the local food bank or homeless shelter. *Boys and girls, today's offering is going to help those in need. Just as the Lord helps those who call out to Him. Christians should help those who need help. Today we're helping the homeless (hungry) at the* _____.

Memory Verse Status: Romans 10:13 *Everyone who calls on the name of the Lord will be saved.*

Memory Verse Talk: (use *The Road* lesson 4, slide A)

Sometimes people are afraid to call out to God. They think God wants to punish them for the bad things they've done. But God loves us. That's why He sent his Son to die on the cross for our sins. When we're in trouble, even if it's our own fault, all we have to do is call on Jesus, and He will forgive us, save us, and help us.

Memory Verse Activity: (use *The Road* lesson 4, slide A)

Have the children read the verse using different voices. For instance, they can say the verse with an English accent, in a squeaky voice, very loud, or whispering. By the time you use 6 or 7 ways to say the verse, they children should know it by heart.

Object Lessons:

1. Object Lesson: Tadpoles and Frogs

Supplies Needed: toy or real frog

This frog wasn't always a frog. At one time it was a tadpole. Over time the tadpole begins to change. It take a while, but when the change is done, the tadpole has become a frog.

There are many differences between a tadpole and a frog. A tadpole has a tail, and a frog doesn't. Tadpoles don't have arms or legs. Frogs have long legs that help them jump. Tadpoles have gills so they breathe under water. Frogs don't have gills. They breathe air through their lungs. Frogs love to swim in the water, but they also like to hop on dry land. Tadpoles have to stay in the water to breathe.

It kind of hard to believe that this frog was once a tadpole, but it was. It went through a change called a metamorphosis.

When we ask Jesus into our hearts as our Savior, we also go through a dramatic change or a metamorphosis, but our change doesn't show on the outside like a tadpole changing into a frog. Our change happens on the inside. We begin to want to do things that will help us grow closer to God, things like praying and going to church. We also start to want to do right. We feel bad when we do something wrong. Those are all inside changes that show we are saved, and that Christ is forming us into a new creation. We are becoming like Him.

2. Story: The Boy Who Cried Wolf

I'm going to tell you a story you've never heard before. It's called the boy who cried Wolf.

When the children protest that they've heard this story, tell them that you want to tell the story anyway.

There once lived a boy who watched his father's sheep. He was bored watching the sheep, so he decided to play a trick on his father. He shouted, "wolf, wolf." The father was afraid for his son and grabbed his rifle to run to where his son was. The son laughed when he saw how his father ran to him. His father warned him never to do that again.

The next day, the boy was bored again. He started thinking about how funny his father looked running out to the field. The father looked so scared. He decided to do it again. He yelled, "wolf, wolf" as loud as he could. The father grabbed the rifle and ran to the field. The boy rolled on the ground laughing at the father. The father again warned the boy not to cry wolf unless there really was a wolf.

The third day, the boy saw a wolf running toward the sheep. He yelled as loud as he could. "Wolf, wolf." What do you think happened?

Let the children tell you how the father didn't listen and the boy was eaten by the wolf.

No, I told you that you've never heard this story before. The father ran to the boy and shot the wolf. The father was like our Heavenly Father. No matter how many times we call out to God, He will answer us and save us. That's because everyone who calls out to the Lord for help will be saved.

Praise and Worship

Bible Story: Paul Makes a U-Turn (Acts 9:1-18)

Supplies Needed: Go sign, Stop sign, Yield sign, U-Turn Sign or *The Road* lesson 4, slides B-E

One man who is mentioned a lot in the New Testament of the Bible is the Apostle Paul. He wrote most of the New Testament, but he wasn't always a great man of God. Before he became Paul, his name was Saul.

Saul was on a mission to kill and imprison as many Christians as he could. He didn't believe Jesus was the Son of God. He thought he was doing God a favor by arresting and hurting anyone who believed on the name of Jesus Christ. That is what they call persecuting Christians.

One day, Saul was on the road to Damascus. He planned to go there to kill Christians, but something happened that stopped him.

(show stop sign) A light shone from Heaven that knocked Saul off his horse and caused him to fall on the ground. A voice from Heaven said, "Saul, Saul, why are you persecuting me."

Saul was scared. He asked the voice who He was. The voice told Saul He was Jesus who Saul had been persecuting. At that point, Saul knew he'd been wrong.

(show U-turn) He decided to make a U-turn and follow Jesus.

Jesus told him what to do. He told him to go to a man named Ananias who was a Christian. When the light went away, Saul was blind. He couldn't see anything. He could have gone to a doctor or had his men lead him home.

(show yield sign) But he yielded to the voice and had his men take him to Ananias.

(show go sign) When Saul went to Damascus, Ananias was told by God to go to Saul. He prayed for Saul and Saul's sight was restored. That's when Saul knew he was to go preach about Jesus to everyone.

Because Saul stopped fighting against God (show stop sign) *and yielding his life to God* (show yield sign), *God sent him to go to the world and preach the Gospel* (show God sign), *and Saul was never the same. He changed his name to Paul and made a U-turn in his life.* (show U-turn)

Message: Making a U-turn

Every one of us can make a U-Turn in our lives. Christ has showed us the way. All we have to do is turn to God and follow the Romans Road to salvation.

We admit that we've sinned.

We see that sin keeps us from God.

We accept that Jesus died on the cross to save us from our sin and raised from the dead to by our Lord and Savior.

We call on the name of Jesus to be saved.

It's that simple.

Talk to the children about how they can tell their friends about Jesus using the Romans Road. Call any children forward who want to be saved and lead them in the sinner's prayer.

Small Group Chat: Salvation

Ask the children if they have been saved. Talk about what salvation means. It's not just saying a few words. It's making a U-turn and changing everything. When we accept Jesus as our Lord, we surrender or yield our lives to Him. Read Romans 12:1-2 to the students.

At this point, you might also want to talk to your students about water baptism. Talk to your pastor about when the next water baptism will be and contact the parents to ask permission for their children be baptized.

The Journey: The Road, Lesson 5

Lesson 5 - The Road to Rome

Focus Point: Jesus wants us to tell people about Him.

Goal: Children will learn how to tell others about how to be saved.

Memory Verse: Romans 10:9 *If you declare with your mouth, "Jesus is Lord," and believe in your heart that God raised him from the dead, you will be saved.*

Supplies Needed:

- *The Journey* Videos (free with registration)
- *The Journey* Jpeg Slides (free with registration)
- Copies of *The Journey* Family Devotional Sheet (free with registration)
- Road Construction Costume: hardhat, yellow or orange caution vest, walkie-talkie
- police puppet or costume
- Go sign from *The Road* lesson 4
- Road Construction Costume: hardhat, yellow or orange caution vest
- wordless book or yellow, black, red, white, and green construction paper with verses written on them
- fishing pole
- yellow, black, red, white, and green beads, and string or cord

Opening: *The Journey Countdown* or *The Road* or *The Journey* Slide (Available free with registration of this curriculum.)

Welcome: Welcome the children and tell them how happy you are to see them. If you have a smaller church, this is the time how their week has been and ask for prayer requests.

Today is our last day on the Romans Road. I hope every one of you has decided to accept Jesus as your Lord, but there are others who need the Lord too. God wants us to share salvation with them.

Prayer: Ask a child to pray over the service.

Rules: (use rules slide)

Go over the *5 Ups Rules*: 1. Sit up straight. 2. Listen up. 3. Hush up. 4. Don't get up and run around or go to the bathroom. 5. Worship Up! (stand and participate during praise and worship)

Theme or Activity Songs: Choose one or two fast moving activity songs that goes with the curriculum.

Memory Verse Skit: (use *The Road* lesson 5, slide A)

Supplies needed: Police officer puppet or person dressed as a police officer

Officer Shalom: Hi boys and girls. One of the saddest calls I ever answered was one that didn't have to turn out the way it did. A woman was in danger because a bad man was trying to break into her house. Police were in the area, but they were never called to her house because she didn't call 9-1-1. If she had called, the bad man wouldn't have been able to break in because the police would have gotten there in time. Nobody knows why she didn't call. The bad man killed her. It was a waste because we could have stopped him. As sad as that is, it's even sadder when people know about how Jesus died to save them, but they never make the decision to be saved. It's so easy, even easier than dialing 9-1-1 because you don't need a phone. Romans 10:9 says "If you declare with your mouth, 'Jesus is Lord,' and believe in your heart that God raised him from the dead, you will be saved."

Game Time: Review Game (use game time slide and *The Road lesson 5* review game jpegs)

You can have children stand if they know the answer or have up to five members on two teams compete against each other. The game will review what the children have learned during *The Road*.

Skit: Ralph the Road Guy – Go

Supplies needed: Road Guy costume, walkie-talkie, Go Sign from *The Road* lesson 4.

Leader: Hello, Ralph. What sign are you hanging up today?

Ralph: I'm pretty excited about this sign. (holds up Go sign) Do you remember, last week, how you told me that anyone who calls on the name of the Lord can be saved?

Leader: Yes, I remember that.

Ralph: Well, I got to thinking I need God in my life, so I did it. I called on Jesus to save me, and He did.

Leader: That's wonderful, Ralph. What does that have to do with your sign?

Ralph: I got to thinking that other people need to learn how to be saved. But they won't know unless we go and tell them.

Leader: So that's why you have a Go sign?

Ralph: That's right. The road crew uses go signs to let traffic through when the have a lane blocked by construction, but I decided to use the Go sign to remind me to go and tell others about how Jesus can save them – just like He did me.

Leader: That's great, Ralph. We're going to talk some more about that today.

Ralph: Maybe I'll stick around and hear more about it.

Offering: *Today, we're going to do something different for offering. In 2 Corinthians 9:7, the Bible says, "God loves a cheerful giver." Today we are going to declare how excited we are to give by shouting "Hallelujah."* Lead the children in shouting Hallelujah several times before taking the offering.

Memory Verse: Romans 10:9 *If you declare with your mouth, "Jesus is Lord," and believe in your heart that God raised him from the dead, you will be saved.*

Memory Verse Talk: (use *The Road* lesson 5, slide A)

Today's verse is Romans 10:9. Repeat it with me. "If you declare with your mouth, 'Jesus is Lord,' and believe in your heart that God raised him from the dead, you will be saved." This verse is important because it tells us how to be saved. It isn't enough to believe Jesus died for our sins. We need to believe in our hearts that Jesus raised from the dead. That means we not only believe it in our minds, we accept Him as our savior in our hearts, and then we say tell people that He is our Lord. That means we tell people that we've given our lives to God.

Memory Verse Activity: Verse Motions

Have children do motions as you review the verse. Do this a couple of times until they learn the motions. Then every time you do this, have them do the motions faster.

If you declare with your mouth (point to mouth)

Jesus is Lord (point up)

And believe in your heart (put hand over heart)

That God (point up)

Raised Him from the dead (raise hand up in sweeping motion)

Then you (point to each other)

Will be saved (put both hands over heart)

Object Lessons:

1. Object Lesson: Wordless Book meets the Romans Road

Supplies Needed: wordless book or yellow, black, red, white, and green construction paper with verses written on them

We've learned 5 verses during this series called The Road. Those verses are sometimes called the Romans Road because they are used to lead people on the road to salvation and because they are all found in the book of Romans. Today, we're going to review those verses along with the Wordless book so that you can share with your friends how to get saved. A Wordless Book is a book with colors instead of words.

Show yellow page.

God lives in Heaven. He loves us and wants us to live forever in Heaven with Him.

Show black page with this verse: *Romans 3:23   For all have sinned and fall short of the glory of God.*

As much as God loves us, there is a problem. God cannot allow sin, and everyone on Earth has sinned.

Show red page with these verses: *Romans 6:23   For the wages of sin is death, but the gift of God is eternal life in Jesus Christ our Lord.*

Romans 5:8   But God demonstrates his own love for us in this: While we were still sinners, Christ died for us.

Even though we've sinned, God loves us so much that He provided a gift for us, a way to salvation. He sent Jesus Christ, His Son, to die on the cross and take the punishment for our sin.

Show white page with these verses: *Romans 10:13   For, "Everyone who calls on the name of the Lord will be saved."*

Romans 10:9   If you use your mouth to say, "Jesus is Lord," and if you believe in your heart that God raised Jesus from death, then you will be saved.

God will force His gift of salvation on anyone, but anyone who calls on the name of the Lord will be saved. All you have to do is believe in your heart that Jesus died for our sins and was raised from the dead and tell people that Jesus is your Lord. That means that you've given your life to Him. It's that simple.

Show the green page.

It doesn't stop there. God wants us to grow closer to Him. We can do that by surrendering our lives to God and yielding to Him in worship. He wants to have a relationship with us. He wants to be our friend and walk through life with us. The closer we grow to God and the more we yield to Him, the closer He will be to us.

2. **Fisher of Men**

Supplies needed: fishing pole

How many of you have ever been fishing? How do you attract fish to your pole? Bait.

God wants us all to be fishermen, but He doesn't want us to catch fish. God wants us to catch people. He wants us to be fishers of men.

That doesn't mean we take a fishing pole and try to catch people with it. What God wants us to do is to tell other about Jesus and how we were saved. We can tell them how they can be saved also.

What do you think we use as bait when we tell others about Jesus? Let the children answer first. *We use our lives. If we're living for God and loving others, people will want to know what is different about us. Then when we tell them about Jesus, they might want to listen.*

Any fisherman can tell you that you won't catch every fish that swims by. That's true when we're telling people about Jesus. Not everyone will want to be saved. We can't force them. All we can do is pray for them and tell them about Jesus. It's up to them to do the rest.

Praise and Worship

Bible Story: Paul Shares the Good News (Acts 13)

After Paul made a U-turn and decided to accept Jesus as his savior, he knew the Christian life doesn't end there. He spent time growing closer to Jesus, but he also went out into the world and became a missionary.

A missionary is somebody who goes to foreign lands and tells people how they can get saved. Someday, some of you might decide to become missionaries to other countries.

This is a good time to introduce a missions' lesson. If you have a missions project for the children, this would be a good place to talk about it.

Message: Go and Share

Telling others about Jesus can be scary, but God promised to help us through the Holy Spirit. He helps us in three ways:

1. *The Holy Spirit empowers us with boldness: If we need boldness to witness, Christ promised the baptism of the Holy Spirit to empower us and make us bold.*

Acts 1:8 *But you will receive power when the Holy Spirit comes on you. Then you will be my witnesses in Jerusalem. You will be my witnesses in all Judea and Samaria. And you will be my witnesses from one end of the earth to the other.*

2. *The Holy Spirit gives us the Words to say: God will give us the right words to say at the right time.*

Matthew 10:19 *...Don't worry about what you will say or how you will say it. At that time you will be given the right words to say.*

3. *Christ will give you the strength you need.*

Philippians 4:13 *I can do everything by the power of Christ. He gives me strength.*

Small Group Chat & Activity:

Supplies Needed: yellow, black, red, white, and green beads, and string or cord

Sometimes it's hard to remember what to say when you want to tell someone how to be saved. That's why we're going to make a Witness bracelet.

Have the children place the beads on the cord in the following order and explain the meaning.

- Yellow – God/Heaven: God loves everyone and wants us to go to Heaven to be with Him forever.
- Black – Sin: All have sinned. God can't allow sin in Heaven.
- Red – Blood: Jesus died on the cross for our sins.
- White – Pure: If we confess our sins and ask Jesus into our hearts, He will save us and give us eternal life.
- Green – Grow: The Christian life doesn't end there. We should do things like pray, read our Bibles, go to church so that we can know God better.

The Journey Part 2: The Bible: Your GPS for Life

Lesson 1: God's Word Guides Our Lives

Psalm 119:105   *Your word is a lamp for my feet, a light on my path.*

Lesson 2: God's Word Points Us to Jesus

2 Timothy 3:15   *You have known the Holy Scriptures since you were a child. The Scriptures are able to make you wise. And that wisdom leads to salvation through faith in Christ Jesus.* (ICB)

Lesson 3: God's Word Keeps Us from Sin

Psalm 119:11   *I have hidden your word in my heart that I might not sin against you.*

Lesson 4: Do What God's Word Says

Romans 10:17   *Do not merely listen to the word, and so deceive yourselves. Do what it says.*

The Bible Your GPS Lesson 1 – God's Word Guides Our Lives

Focus Point: God's Word guides our lives.

Goal: Students will learn that God's Word has instructions that will help them in every area of their lives.

Memory Verse: Psalm 119:105 *Your word is a lamp for my feet, a light on my path.*

Supplies Needed:

- *The Journey* Videos (free with registration)
- *The Journey* Jpeg Slides (free with registration)
- Copies of *The Journey* Family Devotional Sheet (free with registration)
- Road Construction Costume: hardhat, yellow or orange caution vest, walkie-talkie
- police puppet or costume
- Blindfolds
- Rope for the finish line
- Street sign with the name of a nearby street on it – can be made with cardboard
- Marker or chalk board
- Markers or chalk
- Bible
- Crown (you can get a free crown at Burger King or make one out of construction paper)
- Broom
- Compass
- Flashlight or Lantern
- GPS
- Map

Opening: *The Journey Countdown* or *The Bible: Your GPS for Life* or *The Journey* Intro Slide (Available free with registration of this curriculum.)

Welcome: Welcome the children and tell them how excited you to see them. Talk about how of the next 4 lessons will be about the greatest book that ever was – The Bible. The Bible isn't only a book, it's God's Word, and it is the only book that is a GPS for your life.

Prayer: Ask a child to pray over the service.

Rules: (use rules slide)

Go over the *5 Ups Rules*: 1. Sit up straight. 2. Listen up. 3. Hush up. 4. Don't get up and run around or go to the bathroom. 5. Worship Up! (stand and participate during praise and worship)

Theme or Activity Songs: Choose one or two fast moving activity songs that goes with the curriculum.

Memory Verse Skit: The Right Guide (use *The Bible: Your GPS for Life* lesson 1, slide A)

Supplies needed: police officer puppet or uniform

Peace Officer Shalom: Hi boys and girls. I'm Police Officer Shalom. They call me that because I keep the peace by arresting wrong doers. One of my jobs as a police officer is to give warnings to motorists when the lights on their cars aren't functioning properly. Sometimes a headlight, tail light, or brake light burns out and the motorist doesn't know it. I stop the driver and give him a warning that the light needs fixed right away. I don't do that because I want to be mean. Driving a vehicle without the proper lights can be dangerous.

For instance, if a break light is out, the driver in the car behind might not know the motorist has stopped. This could cause an accident. In the evening, if a motorist doesn't have a functioning headlight, he might miss something dangerous in the road ahead and run into it. That's why I give warnings. The Bible is like the lights on our car. It shows us what is ahead, so we won't get into a bad situation. That's why todays verse is so important. Psalm 199:105 says "Your word is a lamp for my feet, a light for my path." Just as lights are important on the road, God's word lights our way in life.

Game Time: Follow the Guide (use *The Journey* game time slide)

Supplies Needed: blindfolds, a rope for the finish line.

Choose 4 students to play the game for 2 pairs of 2. Have a rope at the front of the room where 1 student from each team will stand. The other 2 students will stand at the back of the room. They will be blindfolded and turned around 3 times. The students in the front of the room will guide their partners in the back across the finish line with instructions they call out. The catch is that all of the other students in the room will be yelling instructions at the same time to confuse them. The team with the first student to cross the finish line wins.

Just as these children had to listen carefully for instructions to win this game, we need to listen to the instructions from our guide, the Bible, to navigate through life.

Offering: Explain about what the tithe is. Read Malachi 3:10. *God's Word commands us to pay tithe, but it also says we can test God by paying tithe. When we pay tithe, God will bless us.*

Skit: Street Signs

Supplies Needed: Road Guy costume, walkie-talkie, Street sign with the name of a nearby street on it – can be made with cardboard

Ralph: (Wanders in carrying a street sign) Hi, everybody. I'm all done hanging up the road signs to make people safe. Now I've been assigned to a new job.

Leader: Hi, Ralph. Children, you remember Ralph the Road Guy (Rhonda, the Road Gal). His job is to work on roads to make them safe. It's great to have you back, but I have a question. If you're done hanging up road signs, how come you're carrying a road sign?

Ralph: I'm not carrying a road sign. I'm carrying a street sign.

Leader: (scratches head) Isn't that what I just said?

Ralph: Nope, a road sign and a street sign are two entirely different things. A road sign warns you of the rules of the road, like stop or yield or one-way street. If might tell a driver what the speed limit is or warn him that a road is closed ahead. Road signs keep you safe.

Leader: I understand that, but what I don't get is what makes your street sign different than a road sign.

Ralph: (holds up street sign) A street sign tells you the name of the road. If you didn't have street signs, you'd never know where you were or how to get where you're going. You'd get lost really quick.

Leader: That may have been true in the past, but now everyone has a GPS. The GPS tells me the name of the road and how to get where I'm going.

Ralph: That's where you're wrong. Where do you think the GPS and map making companies find out where the roads are and what they're named?

Leader: I never really thought about it, Ralph. How do they find out?

Ralph: They have these surveyors that go around measuring the roads and mapping them out.

Leader: That makes sense, but what does that have to do with street signs?

Ralph: How do you think they find out the names of the roads?

Leader: The street signs?

Ralph: That's right, the street signs. That's why it's important I get the street signs right. If I make a mistake, your GPS won't direct you the right way. You'll get lost for sure.

Leader: I'm glad God didn't make any mistakes in our GPS for our lives.

Ralph: Our GPS for our lives? I don't know what you're talking about. I never heard of a GPS for your life.

Leader: I'm talking about the Bible. God's Word, the Bible, guides our lives. If we do what it says, we won't get lost or in trouble. God's Word is our GPS for life.

Ralph: Now that makes a lot of sense. Well, I need to go hang up these signs. See you later. (Exits)

Memory Verse: Psalm 119:105 *Your word is a lamp for my feet, a light on my path.*

Memory Verse Talk: (use *The Bible, Your GPS* lesson 1, slide A)

Read the verse. *Have you ever stubbed you toe in the dark? I have, and it hurts. The reason I stubbed my toe was because I didn't have a light to guide my way. Because I didn't have any light, I ran into the dresser. God's Word is described as a lamp that lights our way through our path through life, yet many people don't take the time to see what it says and to let it light their way. They end up hurting themselves in ways far worse than stubbing their toes.*

Memory Verse Activity: Picture Scripture

Supplies needed: marker board and markers or chalk board and chalk

Choose 2 teams of no less than 3 students. Have each team decide a picture to draw about when the Bible could guide their paths. Each team will have one student tell about the picture. You or the students not on any team will judge which team had the best idea not the best picture. If you have time, you could also judge on the best drawing.

Video: Flashlight: This video is included in digital files for The Road available for free when you register this curriculum.

Bible Story: Josiah Finds a Book (2 Kings 22-23)

Supplies Needed: Bible, crown (you can get a free crown at Burger King or make one out of construction paper), broom

Have an eight-year-old come to the front, and place a crown on his head. If you don't have an eight year old student, chose the child closest to that age.

King Josiah became king of Israel in a wicked time. People were offering sacrifices to idols, and they didn't care about God. The Bible wasn't guiding their lives because they didn't even know where it was, and they never read it.

When King Josiah became king, he was only eight years old. Many of you are close to that age. Can you imagine ruling a country at your age? Josiah loved God and wanted to be a good ruler. He did everything he knew to do, but he didn't have the Bible to guide him.

Have the child sweep. *One day, Josiah sent men to clean the temple. They found the Word of God. Josiah read it and became very upset. He realized that he and the people of Israel were not honoring God. He asked God to forgive him, and he brought everyone together to have the Word of God read to them. Then he used the Bible to guide him in ruling Israel. Because of this, he became one of the best kings in Israel.*

Hold up the Bible. *Sometimes we act like we don't have a Bible when we don't read it or find out what it says, but we don't have an excuse like Josiah. Most people in this country has a Bible. (If some of your students don't have a Bible, this would be a good time to pass out Bible for them to keep. There are organizations that sell discounted Bibles for this purpose.)*

When Josiah found the Bible, the first thing he did was to read it. Then he did what it said and used it as a guide for ruling his nation. We need to read the Bible and use it as a guide for ruling our lives. The Bible needs to become our GPS for life.

Praise and Worship:

Object Lessons:

2. God's Word is Our Compass

Supplies needed: compass (One option is to give every child a compass to take home. Companies like Oriental Trading sell toy compasses inexpensively in bulk.)

Hold up the compass. Explain how a compass is an important tool to have if you are hiking in the woods. It has for directions printed on it, but the needle of a compass always points north.

Suppose I was camping in the woods, and I decided to go exploring. After a while, I might lose my sense of direction and not know the way back to the camp site. I know that I hiked north from the camp site, but I don't remember which direction I came from. If I didn't have a compass, I might try the direction I think I came from. If I'm wrong, I'll get further away from the campsite and will be hopelessly lost. If I'm right, I might wander around in a circle instead of going straight south and end up where I started. Either way, I'd be in trouble.

But if I had a compass, I could use it to find my way back. I would turn the compass until the needle pointed toward the N. That would be north. As long as I went the opposite way, I'd know I was going south. I'd be able to find my way back to the campsite.

In life, God has given us a spiritual compass to help us find our way. That compass is the Bible, the Word of God. The Bible has a needle that always points one way just as a compass does. The Bible always points to Jesus. If we use the Bible as our guide and follow Jesus, we won't get lost.

3. God's Word is Our Flashlight

Supplies needed: flashlight or lantern

Have you ever got up in the middle of the night and tried to find your way to the bathroom? Unless you have a night light, turn on a light, or use a flashlight, it's difficult to do. You have to feel your way along the furniture and the walls, and if something is on the floor, you might stub your toe or step on it. Most people don't want to turn on the light in the middle of the night because they might wake other people in the house or because the light is too bright and might hurt their eyes, but some people are smart enough to keep a flashlight by their beds. That way, they can turn on the flashlight and see the step in front of them.

God's Word is like that. It might not show you how to live your entire life, but it shows you what to do next. It lights up the next step to take. For instance, if you see another student being bullied or picked on, you know that God's Word tells you to be kind to one another. That may mean telling a teacher about what is happening or being that student's friend when nobody else will stick up for him.

If somebody tells you to stop praying at lunch during school, you know that God's Word says that if we are ashamed of Him, He will be ashamed of us. That means you should keep praying and explain to the person that told you to stop about why you will continue to pray.

If your best friend stole something from another kid's desk and wants you to do the same, you know from God's Word that stealing is wrong. You know to talk to your friend about stealing and tell her to return what she stole.

If a video game or TV show has something in it that is against God's Word, you know that the Bible says to take every thought captive which means we should turn it off. The Bible guides your steps through life like a flashlight guides your steps in the middle of the night.

Message: God's Word is Our GPS

Supplies needed: GPS (you can use your cell phone), map, Bible

Hold up the Bible. Explain that the Bible is like a GPS for life. It guides us through decisions we make.

Hold up the map. Talk about how when you were young, they didn't have GPSs. People had to use maps. It was difficult because first you would have to find out where you were on the map. Then you'd have to figure out how to get where you were going. Demonstrate.

Sometimes maps didn't work well because the roads would change or there might be a road that was closed, and the map didn't show it. Unfold the map and show how difficult it would be to use while driving.

I'm glad we don't use maps anymore. The GPS is much easier to use.

If you're lost, you can press "Go Home" and the GPS will guide you every step until you're home. If you're spiritually lost, you can turn to John 3:16 or the book of Romans, and the Bible will guide you on how to be saved.

If you don't know which way to turn, the GPS will let you know when to turn right and when to turn left. If we don't know which way to turn in life, we can pray and read God's Word, and it will guide us by giving us wisdom on which way to go.

If there is road construction or congestion up ahead, a GPS will warn the driver. In the same way, God's Word warns us away from danger.

If we want to go in a certain destination, we plug the address into the GPS. The Bible also has addresses.

Show *The Bible: Your GPS for Life* lesson 1, slide b.

The Bible is divided into two major sections. The Old Testament is at the beginning, and the New Testament is at the end. Each section is divided into smaller section with books. In the Bible, an address contains the book of the Bible, the chapter, and the verse. You can find any Bible verse using these addresses.

As great as a GPS is, it won't do you any good unless you turn it on. In the same way, God's Word won't guide your life unless you read it and learn what it says. The take home family devotion sheets are a good place to start. They have Bible addresses of passages that go with each lesson you learn in children's church.

A GPS plugs into a charger so the battery won't die. When you read and study God's Word, you'll want to plug into a spiritual charger by spending time in the presence of God. Then you can ask God to help you understand what He is saying in God's Word and how to apply it to your life.

For response time, lead the children in a prayer or have an altar call. Pray for the children who come forward.

Small Group Chat: God's Word Guides Our Lives

Ask children questions about situations they might be in and how God's Word applies. Be sure to have some verses ready for suggestions.

Here are some questions you can use.

If you see someone being bullied, what should you do?

If your best friend steals something, what should you do?

What should you do if your parents get a divorce?

If you have a hard time with a subject in school, what does God's Word tell you to do?

What should you do if you're afraid?

If you have time, also go over the handout on the books of the Bible and how they are arranged.

The Journey: Your GPS, Lesson 2

The Bible Your GPS Lesson 2: God's Word Points Us to Jesus

Focus Point: Everything in God's Word points to Jesus.

Goal: Children will learn that every book in the Bible is about Jesus.

Memory Verse: 2 Timothy 3:15 (ICB) *You have known the Holy Scriptures since you were a child. The Scriptures are able to make you wise. And that wisdom leads to salvation through faith in Christ Jesus.*

Supplies Needed:

- *The Journey* Videos (free with registration)
- *The Journey* Jpeg Slides (free with registration)
- Copies of *The Journey* Family Devotional Sheet (free with registration)
- Road Construction Costume: hardhat, yellow or orange caution vest, walkie-talkie
- police puppet or costume
- Street signs with names of roads on them – can be made out of cardboard
- Bible
- Optional Object Lesson: 3 Way Bible Coloring Book available at many online retail stores and at magic shops
- *He Is* by Aaron Jeffries (song available through iTunes or on YouTube)
- Storybook
- Stack of letters tied with string

Opening: *The Journey Countdown* or *The Bible: Your GPS for Life* or *The Journey* Intro Slide (Available free with registration of this curriculum.)

Welcome: Welcome the children and ask them what the Bible is about. If one of the students answers Jesus, ask the student if even the Old Testament stories like creation and David and Goliath are about Jesus or only the New Testament. The correct answer is that the whole Bible is about Jesus.

Prayer: Ask a child to pray over the service.

Rules: (use rules slide)

Go over the *5 Ups Rules*: 1. Sit up straight. 2. Listen up. 3. Hush up. 4. Don't get up and run around or go to the bathroom. 5. Worship Up! (stand and participate during praise and worship)

Theme or Activity Songs: Choose one or two fast moving activity songs that goes with the curriculum.

Memory Verse Skit: Laws are About People's Rights (use *The Bible: Your GPS for Life* lesson 1, slide A)

Supplies needed: police officer puppet or uniform

Peace Officer Shalom: Hi boys and girls. I'm Police Officer Shalom. They call me that because I keep the peace by arresting wrong doers. Many people think police officers issue traffic tickets because they like to be mean and boss people around. That couldn't be further from the truth. The reason we have traffic laws like speed limits and legal stops at stop signs is to protect people and their rights. In fact, most laws are written to protect people's rights. Let's take the speed limit. In school zones, the speed limit is 20 miles per hour. If drivers go faster than that, they will endanger children going to school. The law is to protect those children's right to life and safety. Just like most laws are made to protect people's rights, all of God's Word is to show people Jesus, the Son of God. 2 Timothy 3:15 says *"You have known the Holy Scriptures since you were a child. The Scriptures are able to make you wise. And that wisdom leads to salvation through faith in Christ Jesus."* I have to go now so I can protect people's rights.

Game Time: Follow the Guide (use *The Journey* game time slide)

This is a simple game based on the classic childhood game *Going on a Trip*. The first child says, "I'm going on a journey and taking" (something beginning with the letter A). The second child says the same thing but chooses something with the letter B. Continue until you get through the whole alphabet. If a child can't think of something, he is out.

As we go on a journey through the Bible, every story begins and ends with Jesus.

Offering: *Jesus talked about treasure when He was on Earth. He said in Matthew 6:20, "For where your treasure is, there your heart will be also." One reason I give in offering is because I want my heart to be focused on Jesus.*

Skit: All Roads Lead to ...

Supplies needed: Road Guy costume, walkie-talkie, street signs with names of roads on them

Ralph: (Wanders in carrying street signs) I can't stay long today. I'm going to have to work a lot of hours to get done in time.

Leader: What's wrong, Ralph? You look flustered.

Ralph: I am. The new mayor read somewhere about all roads leading to Rome.

Leader: What does that have to do with you being flustered?

Ralph: He decided that all roads should lead to city hall. The problem is all roads don't lead to City Hall. They lead all over the place.

Leader: Well, there's nothing the mayor can do about it now. The roads are already built.

Ralph: That's where I come in, me and the city's whole road crew.

Leader: How does the mayor think you can make all the roads lead to city hall? That's impossible.

Ralph: The mayor says we don't have to make all the roads lead to city hall, but he does say that every road should lead to a road that goes to city hall. And guess who has to make that happen.

Leader: You do?

Ralph: You got it. Me and my crew are working overtime on this one.

Leader: Sounds like a hard job.

Ralph: It is, and not just for us. After the roads are built to connect everything, street signs like these have to be put up, and then the road map people and the GPS makers have to change everything. That doesn't even consider the people whose houses and businesses are in the way of the new roads.

Leader: Sounds like a mess.

Ralph: I tried to tell the mayor that, but he won't listen.

Leader: I'm glad the Bible isn't like that. In the Bible, everything already points to Jesus.

Ralph: Glad to hear it, but I gotta go know. I have tons of work to do.

Leader: I'll pray the mayor changes his mind.

Ralph: I'm praying the same thing. (runs out)

Memory Verse: 2 Timothy 3:15 (ICB) *You have known the Holy Scriptures since you were a child. The Scriptures are able to make you wise. And that wisdom leads to salvation through faith in Christ Jesus.*

Memory Verse Talk: (use *The Bible, Your GPS for Life* lesson 1, slide A)

Some people think the Bible is just a bunch of unrelated stories about God, but it isn't. It's a history book about how God dealt with mankind from the beginning and how Jesus Christ who is God provided salvation for everyone.

Memory Verse Activity: Bible Pass

Supplies needed: Bible open to memory verse

You can use enough students to complete the verse or have every student participate and repeat the verse multiple times. Open the Bible to the memory verse. The first student says the first word of the verse. The second student says the second word. Continue until the whole verse is read. When the activity is over, have all the students say the verse together. If you have younger children who can't read, pair them with older children. Have the older child whisper the word to the younger child. The younger child will then say the word.

Optional Object Lesson: 3 Way Bible Coloring Book Gospel Illusion

Object Lesson and instructions are available on many online retail stores and most magic shops.

Bible Story: He Is

Supplies Needed: Song *He Is* by Aaron Jeffries (video of the song available on YouTube)

Play *He Is* by Aaron Jeffries. You can use a video on YouTube. Before the song, tell how the song points out that Jesus was throughout the Bible. The Bible is about Him.

Praise and Worship

Object Lessons:

1. The Bible is a Storybook

Supplies needed: a well-known fairytale storybook with pictures, the Bible

Show the pictures in the storybook and briefly tell the story.

This story book has a beginning. Most fairytales begin with "Once upon a time…" Then the story goes on to tell about a hero or heroine.

The Bible has a hero too. His story begins with "In the beginning, God created the Heavens and the Earth. Jesus is God, and according to John 1:1, He was there at the beginning creating everything. Jesus is the hero of the Bible. The difference is this storybook is about a make-believe hero. Jesus is a real hero, and this book (hold up the Bible) *is about Him.*

There's a lot of stuff that happens in this storybook (hold up the storybook) *before the end.* Tell some of the things that happen in the story. *But everything that happens is somehow connected to the hero.*

(Hold up the Bible.) *Everything in this book is also connected to the hero of the story, Jesus Christ.*

(Hold up the storybook.) *This storybook has a climax.* Tell about how the hero of the story faced his or her greatest challenge and overcame.

(Hold up the Bible.) *This book also has a climax. Jesus came to Earth to die on the cross for our sins so we could be saved and won the victory by being raised from the dead.*

(Hold up the storybook.) *This storybook also has an ending. It tells what happened as a result of the hero winning the day in the climax and then ends with "They all lived happily ever after."*

(Hold up the Bible.) *This book also has an ending. It shows how the church thrived and is still thriving today. It has a happily ever after part too. In the last chapter of the Book of Revelations, it says "No longer will there be any curse. The throne of God and of the Lamb will be in the city, and his servants will serve him. They will see his face, and his name will be on their foreheads. There will be no more night. They will not need the light of a lamp or the light of the sun, for the Lord God will give them light. And they will reign for ever and ever."*

Jesus Christ is the real hero of history and of the Bible, and we are living out His story. One day, He will come again, and we will all live happily ever after. His story isn't done yet. That's why the last verses in Revelation tell us to watch for His returning. "He who testifies to these things says, 'Yes, I am coming soon.' Amen. Come, Lord Jesus. The grace of the Lord Jesus be with God's people. Amen."

Now that's a real happy ending to the greatest story ever told.

2. Love Letters

Supplies needed: a stack of letters tied with a string

Before email became so popular, people would write letters on paper, stick them in an envelope, and mail them. Have any of you ever written a letter to someone and mailed it?

When I was dating, my spouse/boyfriend/girlfriend used to write me love letters with all kinds of mushy things in them. These are the letters, but I'm not going to read them to you. They are very important to me, so I save them in a special box. Sometimes I'll get them out and read them. They remind me how much my spouse/boyfriend/girlfriend loves me. I would never get rid of them.

Long ago, before your parents and grandparents were born, there was a great war called World War II. Almost all of the young men went overseas to fight in this war. They left their girlfriends and wives behind because an evil dictator was trying to take over the world, and they were sent to stop him. That dictator was Hitler.

The men sent overseas must have been lonely because they wrote thousands of love letters to the people they cared about. Many of those love letters are still around. Here's part of one of them.

```
October 23, 1943

Dear Anne,

Just received your letter of Sept. 16, which increased my morale greatly.

I would love to be with you and prove to you that you aren't suffering from
any delusions. If my letters have failed to convey that I do miss you and are
constantly thinking of you I am sorry. Most of my letters are always cut and
dry.

While in the hospital I received your package of Yardley's soap, which is
quite a rarity over here. Thanks for the package. Send some snapshots of
yourself in your next letter. I would love to see the movie roll we took in
New York, my sister said it was good.

Today the weather is perfect for a football game.
Someday we will be able to see some good game together. Will close honey for
now.

With all my love,
Mitch
```

The letter doesn't just have mushy stuff. It also tells what Mitch is going through. Mitch wrote his girlfriend who would later become his wife about things that happened and how he felt about it because he wanted her to know him better.

Hold up Bible.

These are God's love letters to us. He tells us how much He loves us in these letters, but He also tells us what He has been doing throughout history. It also talks about who He is and what He wants. He wants us to know Him better by reading these love letters.

How would Mitch feel if Ann had never read his letters? He would think she didn't really care about him. I wonder if God feels the same way when we don't read His love letters to us.

Message: The Bible Leads Us to Jesus

This is an outline of a children's sermon you can deliver in your own words.

Why the Bible is important:

The Bible is our spiritual bread. (John 6:32-35) Just as we need food every day to nourish our physical bodies, we need God's Word every day to nourish us spiritually. When we feed ourselves by reading God's Word, we're also feeding ourselves on Jesus because He is the bread of life.

The Bible gives revelation and direction. The entire book of Proverbs teaches us how to be wise.

The Bible shows us what is right and what is wrong. If we study the Bible, it will guide us about how we should live. We won't have to wonder what is right or what is wrong because the Bible gives us principles to live by.

The most important thing is that the Bible leads us to Jesus. Quote the memory verse.

If we want to know Jesus, we need to read God's Word.

For response time, lead the children in a prayer or have an altar call and pray for the children who come forward.

Small Group Chat:

The entire Bible is about Jesus. Ask your students how each of these stories is really about Jesus.

Creation: Jesus created all things according to John 1:2-3.

Adam and Eve sinning in the garden: God told the serpent (devil) that Eve's seek would crush him although he would bruise his heel. That seed is Jesus who came to die on the cross for our sins. He won victory over the devil.

Promise to Abraham: God promised Abraham that the world would be blessed through his descendant. That decedent was Jesus.

David and Goliath: David defeated Goliath through the power of God. Jesus defeated the devil. Through His name, we can defeat the giants in our lives.

Jonah and the Big Fish: Just as Jonah was in the belly of a big fish for three days before he was spit up on dry land, Jesus was in the grave for three days before He rose again.

Lesson 3 – God's Word Keeps Us from Sin

Focus Point: God's Word keeps us from sin.

Goal: Students will learn that the Bible teaches us right from wrong, and the more we know the Bible, the less likely we are to sin.

Memory Verse: Psalm 119:11 *I have hidden your word in my heart that I might not sin against you.*

Supplies Needed:

- *The Journey* Videos (free with registration)
- *The Journey* Jpeg Slides (free with registration)
- Copies of *The Journey* Family Devotional Sheet (free with registration)
- Road Construction Costume: hardhat, yellow or orange caution vest, walkie-talkie
- police puppet or costume
- Index cards or card stock
- Marker
- Scotch tape or tack
- Marker board or cork board
- place cards or posters with "Desire", "Pride", and "Sight" on one side of each card and "It is Written" on the other side
- toy sword
- Small Group Chat: small poster board and index cards for each child

Opening: *The Journey Countdown* or *The Bible: Your GPS for Life* or *The Journey* Intro Slide (Available free with registration of this curriculum.)

Welcome: Welcome the children. Talk to them about how everyone knows some things are right and some things are wrong even if they don't believe in God. For instance, everyone knows murder is wrong, but there are some things people disagree on as far as right or wrong. The Bible is the standard for what is right and what is wrong because God rules the universe, so He gets to decide.

Prayer: Ask a child to pray over the service.

Rules: (use rules slide)

Go over the *5 Ups Rules*: 1. Sit up straight. 2. Listen up. 3. Hush up. 4. Don't get up and run around or go to the bathroom. 5. Worship Up! (stand and participate during praise and worship)

Theme or Activity Songs: Choose one or two fast moving activity songs that goes with the curriculum.

Memory Verse Skit: Arresting Wrong Doers (use *The Bible, Your GPS for Life* lesson 3, slide A)

Supplies needed: police officer puppet or uniform

Peace Officer Shalom: Hi boys and girls. I'm Police Officer Shalom. They call me that because I keep the peace by arresting wrong doers. Wrong doers are people who break the law. They murder, steal, use drugs, drink and drive, or commit other crimes that hurt people and are against the law. I follow the law to know who is doing wrong and needs to be arrested. The law tells me what is legally right and wrong.

In the same way, the Bible is like a law book. It tells what is morally right and wrong. If we want to do right, we need to read the Bible often to know what God's moral law is and how to follow it. Psalm 119:11 says, "I have hidden your word in my heart that I might not sin against you." I have to go know so I can arrest more law breakers.

Game Time: The Bible Says (use *The Journey* game time slide)

This is the classic game of Simon Says only using the Bible Says instead. Give children instructions. If you say the Bible Says, they must follow the instructions or they're out. If you don't say the Bible Says, and they follow the instructions, then they're out. Play the game until only one person is standing.

Of course, the Bible doesn't tell you to do all these silly things, but it is the instruction book we should follow. A lot of people use all kinds of different guides to decide what is right and what is wrong, but the Bible is the only guide that tells you the truth about what is sin and how to please God and do right. We should only follow what the Bible says.

Offering:
The Bible says a lot about giving. 2 Corinthians 9:7 says, "Each of you should give what you have decided in your heart to give, not reluctantly or under compulsion, for God loves a cheerful giver." So in this verse, the Bible says we should give what we have decided to give, but we should give it with a cheerful attitude, not because we have to. Let's do that today by clapping when I say, "It's offering time." Lead the children in applause.

Skit: Above the Law

Supplies needed: Road Guy costume, walkie-talkie

Ralph: (Wanders in whistling or humming.)

Leader: You look happy today, Ralph.

Ralph: I am happy. It's a beautiful day, and all is right with the world.

Leader: So, what's happening that has you in such a good mood? Last week, you were so upset after the mayor wanted you to make all those new roads.

Ralph: The city architects and planners got involved. They told the mayor he couldn't do what he was planning.

Leader: He sure seemed to think he could do it last week. How did they change his mind?

Ralph: They told him that a lot he wanted to do was against the law, at least the way he planned to do it.

Leader: Against the law?

Ralph: That's right. Whenever you want to create a new road in this city, the law says it has to be approved by a planning committee. Then you have to get permits. And if the road disrupts businesses, they have a right to go to court and try to block the road being built even if the planning committee approves it. The mayor would have to prove that it's more important to the city to build the road than save the business.

Leader: Didn't the mayor get any of this approved before he gave the orders to build the roads?

Ralph: No, he didn't.

Leader: Wow, it sounds like a lot more people than just the road crews are mad at him.

Ralph: You got that right. The city planning commission, the businesses involved, the architects, the city council, even some of the judges in the city. One judge said that just because he's the mayor doesn't mean he's above the law.

Leader: That's true. Even the president of the United States isn't above the law. Nobody is.

Ralph: The mayor finally got that through his head. He still wants to change the roads in the city, but this time he plans to do it the right way.

Leader: That reminds me of what we're learning today. God's law is in the Bible. It is the standard that teaches us right from wrong.

Ralph: And just like the mayor isn't above the law, nobody is above God's law.

Leader: That's right, Ralph.

Ralph: Well, I need to go now. The mayor has given his road crew the day off, and I have plans with my family. Bye, everyone. (Exits)

Memory Verse: Psalm 119:11 *I have hidden your word in my heart that I might not sin against you.*

Memory Verse Talk: (use *The Bible: Your GPS for Life* lesson 3, slide A)

One way we can make it easier to not sin against God is to memorize Scripture. When we read what the Bible says and memorize it, it gets down into our hearts. When we have God's Word in our hearts, we'll be more likely to do what is right and to avoid what is wrong.

Memory Verse Activity: Memory Verse Scramble

Supplies needed: index cards or card stock, marker, scotch tape or tack, marker board or cork board

Write each word of the verse and the verse address on 2 sets of separate cards. Have a board for children to hang the verse using scotch tape or tacks. Have two teams. Mix up each set and throw it on the floor in front of the board. Each team will have to find the words of the verse and hang them on the board. To make it harder, have the children hang the words in order. Whoever arranges the set into the memory verse first wins.

Bible Story: Jesus Uses God's Word to Resist Sin (Matthew 11)

Supplies needed: place cards or posters with "Desire", "Pride", and "Sight" on one side of each card and "It is Written" on the other side.

Everyone gets tempted to do wrong things, but did you know that even Jesus, the Son of God was tempted by the devil to sin. He was tempted in three ways. Those three ways are the ways we are all tempted to sin. The difference is Jesus didn't fall into those temptations. He used what was written in the Bible to resist them.

Hold up Desire sign.

The first way Jesus was tempted was with desire. Satan sometimes uses our desires, sometimes even good desires like hunger, to get us to sin. Jesus went to the wilderness to fast for 40 days. Fasting is going without food. He did that to prepare for His ministry. The first thing Satan tried to get Jesus to do was to turn stones into bread and eat them. Jesus was hungry, but He knew it was important for Him to finish His fast.

Turn card over.

Jesus fought the temptation to give into desire by saying, "It is written: 'Man shall not live on bread alone, but on every word that comes from the mouth of God.'" He defeated desire by quoting God's Word.

Hold up Pride sign.

Satan also tried to tempt Jesus with pride. He told Jesus that if He was the Son of God, He could throw Himself off a cliff and angels would protect Him. Jesus knew He was God's son, but He didn't let his pride convince Him to try to prove it to the devil.

Turn card over.

Instead Jesus quoted the Bible. "It is also written: 'Do not put the Lord your God to the test.'"

Hold up Sight sign.

One of the greatest temptations we have is wanting what we see. Satan took Jesus to a high mountain and showed Him all the kingdoms of the world and all their riches. He told Jesus he would give him everything he saw if Jesus would bow down to him.

Turn card over.

Jesus defeated that temptation too by using the Bible. Jesus said to him, "Away from me, Satan! For it is written: 'Worship the Lord your God, and serve him only."

When Jesus used the Bible to defeat these temptations, the Bible says the devil left him. When we hide God's Word in our hearts, God's Word will keep us from sin just like it did Jesus.

Praise and Worship

Object Lessons:

1. God's Word is a Sword

Supplies needed: toy sword

The Bible says God's Word is like a sword. It is sharper than a two-edged sword, but it's not meant to hurt other people. It cuts down lies that would try to get us to sin. It cuts the devil down to size when he tempts us just like Jesus used the Word of God to defeat the devil when he tempted Him. It is part of the armor of God and protects us by against anything that would try to destroy us spiritually. The Bible also says it sharp enough to cut into our souls and reveal thoughts and attitudes that might cause us to sin.

The Word of God is powerful and sharp like a sword, but can you imagine a warrior in Bible times going out to battle without his sword? It wouldn't matter how sharp and powerful his sword was, he would be defeated and maybe even killed. That reminds me of the way most Christians are. They battle temptation every day without their sword, God's Word.

Now we can't take our Bible with us everywhere. Even if we did, sometimes it would be hard to look up the right Bible verse to defeat a temptation. That's why we need to put God's Word in our hearts where we can get to our sword at any time. The way to do that is by reading the Bible, listening to teaching about the Bible, and memorizing verses in the Bible. That way, we always have our sword when we need it.

For younger children who can't read yet, let them know about a Bible app that reads the Bible to them. You Version.

2. God's Word is a Vaccination

Supplies needed: use *The Bible: Your GPS for Life* lesson 3, slide B

Have any of you ever seen God's Word in someone's heart? By that, I mean have you ever seen a surgeon open up somebody's chest, and a Bible came out of their heart? That would be silly. Of course, nobody ever hides God's Word in their physical hearts. So, what does the memory verse mean when it talks about hiding God's Word in your heart?

God's Word is a lot like a vaccination. Raise your hands if you've ever received a vaccination. When you are vaccinated, they pump something in you to cause antibodies to form. These antibodies are so small they can't be seen, but they are powerful. When a disease attacks, those antibodies protect the body.

When you hide God's Word in your heart, you learn God's Word consistently. You won't be able to see it, and you won't even realize how powerful it is until you need it. It becomes like a vaccination against sin.

Message:

Hiding God's Word in your heart is easy, but it takes time and diligence.

First, you learn God's Word by reading it or listening to it. If you are too young to read or have reading difficulties, ask you parents to get you a Bible app with audio or to read the Bible to you.

Second, we hide God's Word in our hearts by listening to Bible teachers in church and to our parents as they teach us about the Bible.

The third way is to memorize Scripture. Every week, we give you a memory verse and a take-home paper. If you memorize every verse, within a year, you'll know 52 memory verses. In two years, you'll know 104 memory verses. That's a good start to hiding God's Word in your hearts.

Another good way to put God's Word in your heart is to read the verses on the handout every week. Before long, God will bring to your memory different things the Bible says about what you're going through.

For response time, lead the children in a prayer or have an altar call and pray for the children who come forward. Have the children pledge to start reading the Bible every week.

Small Group Chat:

Supplies needed: small poster board and index cards for each child

We're going to work on a Bible passage and how to hide that Scripture in our hearts.

You can use any Bible passage for this small group chat. I suggest a passage that is longer than today's memory verse such as Psalm 119:9-16 (includes memory verse), Psalm 23, Psalm 100, or John 3:16-21. Tell the children that you'll give them some ideas for memorizing the passage you have chosen. Here are some of those ways:

Have the children write the passage on a poster board and decorate it. Encourage the children to hang the posters on their bedroom doors or walls. Every day, before they go to school, they can read the passage out loud.

Have the children write each verse of the passage on a separate index card. They can learn one verse at a time by having the index card in a place where they see it often.

Have the children make up motions for the verses in the passage. Rehearse the motions so they can use them at home.

Have the children make up a rap or song for the passage.

The Bible: Your GPS for Life Lesson 4 – Do What God's Word Says

Focus Point: Don't just learn God's Word; do what it says.

Goal: Students will learn that they need to do what God's Word says to be blessed.

Memory Verse: James 1:22 *Do not merely listen to the word, and so deceive yourselves. Do what it says.*

Supplies Needed:

- *The Journey* Videos (free with registration)
- *The Journey* Jpeg Slides (free with registration)
- Copies of *The Journey* Family Devotional Sheet (free with registration)
- Road Construction Costume: hardhat, yellow or orange caution vest, walkie-talkie
- police puppet or costume
- Mirror
- Live cut flower in a water vase

Opening: *The Journey* Countdown or *The Bible: Your GPS for Life* or *The Journey* Intro Slide (Available free with registration of this curriculum.)

Welcome: Welcome the children and tell them how excited you to see them. Review the past 4 weeks.

Prayer: Ask a child to pray over the service.

Rules: (use rules slide)

Go over the *5 Ups Rules*: 1. Sit up straight. 2. Listen up. 3. Hush up. 4. Don't get up and run around or go to the bathroom. 5. Worship Up! (stand and participate during praise and worship)

Theme or Activity Songs: Choose one or two fast moving activity songs that goes with the curriculum.

Memory Verse Skit: Obey the Law (use *The Bible: Your GPS for Life* lesson 4, slide A)

Supplies needed: police officer puppet or uniform

Peace Officer Shalom: Hi boys and girls. I'm Police Officer Shalom. They call me that because I keep the peace by arresting wrong doers. One day, I arrested someone for robbing a house. I saw the man taking a television set out to his truck. I knew it wasn't his because the owner of the house called the police to report the burglary.

After I arrested the suspect, he told me that I should let him go. He told me he studied law before he dropped out of school and he knew all the statutes on burglary probably better than I did. Because he had studied the law, he thought I should let him go.

I tried not to laugh at what he was saying, but I couldn't help myself. He thought because he knew the law, he was okay. I instructed him that knowing the law isn't enough. You have to obey the law, or I'll arrest you. I handcuffed him and took him to jail. He tried telling the judge the same thing, and the judge laughed too. The burglar is now serving a prison sentence for his crime.

That sort of reminds me of some Christians. They know what God's Word says, but they don't do what it says. James 1:22 say "Do not merely listen to the word, and so deceive yourselves. Do what it says."

Game Time: Pastor May I (use game time slide)

This game is based on the childhood game, "Mother May I". Children start at the back of the room. You will instruct each child to take two steps forward, hop one step, etc. The child has to say "Pastor May I" or that child has to return to the back of the room.

Whenever we take a step in life, we should do what God's Word says. It's important to not only know God's Word, we need to do God's Word.

Offering: *In God's Word, it says that if we give generously, we will be blessed. Proverbs 11:5 says, "A generous person will prosper; whoever refreshes others will be refreshed." That makes me want to give generously.*

Skit: Building a Foundation
Supplies needed: Road Guy costume, walkie-talkie,

Ralph: (comes in excited) You'll never guess what happened.

Leader: Is it about the road project the mayor wanted?

Ralph: That's right.

Leader Didn't the mayor want all the roads in town to go lead to City Hall?

Ralph: Yep, but the courts told him he couldn't do it without getting the proper permits and having the city council vote for it.

Leader: If I remember right, the mayor said he'd follow the law and have the roads built the right way.

Ralph: That's what he said, but he didn't follow the law. He ordered the construction crew to get busy on the roads right away.

Leader: Wow, what did your boss say to that?

Ralph: My boss told him he wasn't going to order any man on his crew to break the law.

Leader: Then what happened?

Ralph: The mayor fired him and put me in charge. I told the mayor that I wouldn't do it either, and he fired me. Turns out the whole road crew got fired before it was over.

Leader: Oh no, Ralph. Does that mean you have to look for another job?

Ralph: Maybe, but I'm still glad I obeyed God by obeying the law. Besides, everything worked out great.

Leader: All those men are without work. How can you say everything worked out?

Ralph: The city council heard what happened, and now the mayor lost his job too. We're going to have a new mayor who obeys the laws. Not only that, the road project is off.

Leader: That's wonderful. It's important to have a mayor who not only knows the law but obeys the law.

Ralph: That's important when you're a Christian too. You not only need to know what the Bible says, you need to do what it says. That's why I said no to the mayor.

Leader: We're learning about that in children's church today.

Ralph: Awesome. I have to go know. I need to fill out some job applications so I can get a new job. (exits)

Memory Verse: James 1:22 *Do not merely listen to the word, and so deceive yourselves. Do what it says.*

Memory Verse Talk: (use *The Bible: Your GPS for Life* lesson 4, slide A)

Have any of you ever told your parents you would do something then never did it? That's what today's verse is about. Some people know what the Bible says, they know what they should do, but they don't do it. Our memory verse says that people like that are only deceiving themselves. They aren't really obeying God.

Memory Verse Activity: Quote the Verse If...

Call out didn't things that might apply to some of the children. Every child it applies to must jump up and quote the verse. Some ideas to call out are:

- If you brushed your teeth today
- If you are wearing blue
- If you have brown hair
- If you ate breakfast today

Bible Story: Two Brothers (Matthew 21:28-32)

Choose two children to be your illustrations. Tell them to act out what you say.

Jesus told a story about two sons.

Point to the child on your left. *A father asked the first son to work in the vineyard picking grapes. In today's world, he might have asked him to rake the leaves or loose grass in the yard. The first son said, "Of course I will." The father went away, the son didn't bother to take care of the yard work. Maybe he was too busy playing video games or his friends came over to play a game of baseball. Whatever the reason, the boy didn't do what the father asked.*

Point to the child on the right. *When the father got home, he went to the other son and asked him to rake the yard the first son never bothered to rake. The second son said he didn't want to do that. It was too hot, and he'd rather play video games. The father left again, and the second son felt bad about what he'd said. He knew he should obey his father. He went outside a raked the yard all day. When the father came home, he was excited about what a good job the second son had done.*

Jesus asked a question at the end of the story. Which son did what the father wanted? (allow children to answer) *In the same way, the one who does what God wants isn't the one who knows what God's Word says and doesn't do it. The child of God who does the will of God is the one who obeys God's Word.*

Praise and Worship

Object Lessons:

1. Mirror, Mirror on the Wall

Supplies needed: a mirror

I have a mirror here. How many of you look in a mirror when you're getting dressed in the morning? Most people, when they look in the mirror, they fix their hair or wipe toothpaste off their mouth. Most women use a mirror when they apply make-up. What would you think if somebody with their hair messed up and toothpaste on their cheek looked in the mirror but didn't bother to fix their hair or wipe away the toothpaste? That person just walked away from the mirror looking like a mess.

That would be silly, but some Christians do the same thing. The Bible says it is like a mirror that people can look into to see their spiritual lives, but if they see something wrong and don't do what the Bible says about it, it's like they are looking a mirror and ignoring what it shows. The Bible says people like this deceive themselves into thinking they are doing good and obeying God when they are really going against what God's Word says.

2. Attached to the Vine

Supplies needed: live cut flower in a water vase

We've been talking a lot about obeying God's Word, but we all have a hard time obeying God's Word at times. No matter how much we want to do right, we end up doing wrong. So how do I do what God wants?

This flower used to be attached to a plant or bush. Isn't it pretty? It smells pretty too. I put it in water to help it live. I want to keep it forever. How long do you think this flower will live? A couple of days? A week? A year? The truth is this flower will probably not even last a couple of days before it starts to die. Within a week, it will wither away, but the other flowers on the plant will continue to live and be pretty for a long time.

I'm taking care of this flower. I put it in water. I even gave it plant food. So why won't this flower live like the other flowers? The other flowers are attached to the vine or plant they grew on. That plant gives them the nourishment they need. No matter how hard we try, we can't give this flower what it needs to live.

It's the same way with doing what God wants. The Bible calls it abiding in the vine. When we stay attached to God, when we spend time in His presence, it will be easier to obey God's Word.

You can read the Bible and it doesn't help, but when you read the Bible because you want to be close to God and know what He wants to tell you, you'll be able to do what God's Word says. If we want to obey God's Word, we need to stay attached to God.

Message: Blessings that Come with Obedience

Some people think God's Word is full of rules because God wants to control us and make us miserable, but the truth is God wants to bless us. When we obey Him, our lives will be better.

Obeying God's Word protects us. There are bad things that happen to those who do wrong. Have the children name bad things that happen when people do wrong things. *If we obey God, we don't have to worry about those bad things happening to us. God will protect us. If we do wrong, we can ask God's forgiveness knowing He will forgive us and help us obey Him in the future.*

Obeying God's Word shows us we love God. The Bible says that those who love God will obey Him. So, we can make sure we love God by how much we are obeying Him. If we fail in any area, we can ask God to help us love Him more.

Obeying God's Word helps us pray for what we need. John 3:22 says "And whatsoever we ask, we receive of Him, because we keep His commandments, and do those things that are pleasing in His sight." That means we can trust God to answer our prayers because we are in a relationship with Him. When we disobey His Word, it hurts out relationship with God.

If you haven't been obeying God's Word in some area, ask God to forgive you and to help you stay more attached to Him so that you will obey Him.

For response time, lead the children in a prayer or have an altar call and pray for the children who come forward.

Small Group Chat:

Ask this question as a discussion starter.

The closer we are connected with God, the easier it will be to do what God's Word says. The first way we connect to God is to give our lives to Him so He can save us from our sins. If we don't do that, it doesn't matter how much we read the Bible or obey it. What are some of the other ways we can stay connected to God?

Possible answers: worship, prayer, Bible reading, going to church, yielding to God.

The Journey Part 3: City on a Hill

Lesson 1: Our Foundation

Matthew 6:33 *But seek first his kingdom and his righteousness, and all these things will be given to you as well.*

Lesson 2: The Wise Builder

Matthew 7:24 *Therefore everyone who hears these words of mine and puts them into practice is like a wise man who built his house on the rock.*

Lesson 3: Building Materials

Matthew 5:14 *You are the light that gives light to the world. A city that is built on a hill cannot be hidden.*

Lesson 4: Letting Your Light Shine

Matthew 5:16 *In the same way, you should be a light for other people. Live so that they will see the good things you do. Live so that they will praise your Father in heaven.*

The Journey: City on a Hill, Lesson 1

City on a Hill Lesson 1 – Our Foundation

Focus Point: The foundation comes first

Goal: Students will learn that everything in their lives should be built on the foundation of Jesus Christ.

Memory Verse: Matthew 6:33 *But seek first his kingdom and his righteousness, and all these things will be given to you as well.*

Supplies Needed:

- *The Journey* Videos (free with registration)
- *The Journey* Jpeg Slides (free with registration)
- Copies of *The Journey* Family Devotional Sheet (free with registration)
- Road Construction Costume: hardhat, yellow or orange caution vest, walkie-talkie
- police puppet or costume
- A decks of cards
- Marker or bulletin board
- Two sets of papers with words written on them
- Scotch tape
- pearl (you can use a marble or something that resembles a pearl)
- Lego house
- Jewelry
- Cell phone
- Action figure
- Play money
- Canning jar or large glass jar with lid or a large round Rubbermaid container
- Large rocks
- Pebbles
- Sand
- Binoculars
- Magnifying glass
- Bible
- Small Group Discussion: small objects
- Optional Object Lesson: play money, video game or movie DVD, iPhone, football or sports item, glamor magazine or picture of a movie star, math or science book

Opening: *The Journey* Countdown or *City on a Hill* or *The Journey* Intro Slide (Available free with registration of this curriculum.)

Welcome: Welcome the children and tell them how excited you to see them. Talk about how your so excited because of the next 4 lessons, you and the children will be building a city on a hill. The exciting part is that your life is the city you'll be building.

Prayer: Ask a child to pray over the service.

Rules: (use rules slide)

Go over the *5 Ups Rules*: 1. Sit up straight. 2. Listen up. 3. Hush up. 4. Don't get up and run around or go to the bathroom. 5. Worship Up! (stand and participate during praise and worship)

Theme or Activity Songs: Choose one or two fast moving activity songs that goes with the curriculum.

Memory Verse Skit: Building Codes (use *City on a Hill* lesson 1, slide A)

Supplies needed: police officer puppet or uniform

Peace Officer Shalom: Hi boys and girls. I'm Police Officer Shalom. They call me that because I keep the peace by arresting wrong doers. Not all laws concern people doing things like stealing or murdering or even speeding. Some laws are to keep people safe. One example is building codes. These are laws about how to build structures like houses, malls, and office buildings. One of the most important of these codes is about how to build a foundation. Once a building is built nobody thinks about the foundation it's built on. But foundations are more important than anything else in the building. Everything is built on a foundation. If it is strong, the building will be safe. But if the foundation is weak, everything built on it will crumble. Jesus is the foundation we should build our lives one. Every other foundation will crumble. That's the reason for today's memory verse. Matthew 6:33 says *"But seek first his kingdom and his righteousness, and all these things will be given to you as well."* If we seek Jesus and His kingdom first, we'll have a strong foundation to build our lives on.

Game Time: House of Cards (use game time slide)

Supplies Needed: decks of cards

Choose four students to build a house of cards each. Older students would work better for this game. If you have mostly younger children, use different size blocks. They can start together holding up the first four cards. Then each child takes a turn until the house of cards falls.

One reason a house of cards falls so easily is because it doesn't have a firm foundation. We need a firm foundation to build our lives on just as a house needs a firm foundation.

Offering: *Some people use money as a foundation to build their lives on, but money is a weak foundation. When a rich ruler came to Jesus and asked what he must do to be saved. Jesus told him to sell everything he had and follow him. The ruler was sad because he'd built his life on things. He went away and didn't follow Jesus, the only foundation that would have lasted.*

Skit: Building a Foundation

Supplies needed: Road Guy costume, walkie-talkie

Ralph: (Runs in excited) I can only stay a moment, but I was so excited I had to tell you. I got a new job.

Leader: That's wonderful, Ralph. What kind of job is it?

Ralph: I'm working with a construction crew for the city development team. I'll be working on some new sky-scrapers downtown.

Leader: That sounds like a big job.

Ralph: It is, but it's an important one. First, we have to lay the foundations for all of the new buildings. If we don't do this right, it could mean disaster.

Leader: Don't you just have to pour a cement floor for the foundation? Why is it so important?

Ralph: The foundation is what supports the whole building. It's more than just pouring some cement. We need cement and steel girders that go deep into the ground. The larger the building, the stronger the foundation needs to be.

Leader: What kind of disaster could happen if you don't have a strong enough foundation?

Ralph: The building might look good on the inside, but if it doesn't have a strong enough foundation, it might collapse at any moment. Those sky-scrapers have a lot of people in them. If the building collapses during the day, all those people could be hurt or killed not to mention debris falling on the roads near the building or people walking by. The foundation is more important than any other part of the project.

Leader: That sounds like what the Bible says about our lives. We need to build our lives on Jesus. He's our foundation.

Ralph: I never thought of it like that.

Leader: The Bible talks about how our lives are like a city on a hill that shines for all to see if we build our lives on Jesus.

Ralph: So, the Bible talks about building projects too.

Leader: Yes, but our city on a hill is a spiritual city we build inside. Hey, I just thought of something. Since you're not doing roadwork anymore, you won't be Ralph the Road Guy.

Ralph: Nope, now I'm Ralph, the Builder Guy.

Leader: Your new name suits you.

Ralph: I have to go now. I need to get to the job site. (Exits)

Memory Verse: Matthew 6:33 *But seek first his kingdom and his righteousness, and all these things will be given to you as well.*

Memory Verse Talk: (use *City on a Hill* lesson 1, slide A)

Foundations are important. Everywhere we go, buildings are resting on foundations. This church building has a foundation. Your houses or apartment buildings have foundations. If a foundation isn't strong enough, the whole building will eventually collapse.

It's important to have a strong spiritual foundation as well. When we seek God's kingdom first and build our lives on Jesus Christ, He is the foundation that will hold us up in life.

Memory Verse Activity: Seek the Verse

Supplies Needed: marker or bulletin board, two sets of papers with words written on them, scotch tape

Place each word of the verse on a separate piece of paper. Also write various words that are not in the memory verse. Make 2 sets. Place the two sets of words into two mixed-up piles. Divide the children into two teams, one for each pile. Explain to them that not every word in the pile is in the verse. They need to seek out the right words and tape the verse onto the marker board or bulletin board. Whoever arranges the set into the memory verse first wins.

Bible Story: A Pearl of Great Price (Matthew 13:44-46)

Supplies Needed: pearl (you can use a marble or something that resembles a pearl), Lego house, jewelry, cell phone, action figure, play money

Use children to act out this story while you are telling it. The actors you will need are the man who found the pearl, neighbor who owned the land, the person who bought the house, the person who bought the jewelry, the person who bought the cell phone, the person who bought the action figure, the person who bought the pearl. If you have a small ministry, you can combine actors' parts.

Once there was a man who was helping his neighbor dig up his field. While he was digging, he found a pearl of great price. Have the man who found the pearl act like he is digging and finds the pearl.

He was so overjoyed that he jumped up and down. He hid the pearl under a rock. Have the man who found the pearl jump up and down and hide the pearl.

But he had a problem. He didn't own the land. The pearl really belonged to his neighbor. He asked his neighbor if he could by the field. The neighbor told him how much it cost, and it was a lot of money. Have the man who found the pearl ask the neighbor. The neighbor shakes his head no and rubs his fingers together like he wants more money.

The man was sad because he didn't have that much money, but he had an idea. He sold his house and furniture to someone. Have the man sell the Lego house to the house buyer. The house buyer gives him some play money.

Then he took the money to the neighbor and asked if he would accept what he had. The neighbor said he need the full amount. Have the man bring the money to the neighbor. The neighbor shakes his head no and says not enough.

The man still didn't have enough, so he sold all of his wife's jewelry. The man sells the jewelry to the jewelry buyer.

His wife was mad at him, but he still didn't have enough, so he sold all his electronic equipment: his cell phone, computer, IPad, TV, even his iPod. Have the man sell the iPhone to the iPhone buyer.

When he counted the money, he was still sad. He needed more money. He had one thing left to sell, his prize action figures he'd been collecting since he was young. He loved those action figures, but he knew they were worth a lot of money to collectors, so he sold his prize possession. It was hard to part with them, but he wanted the pearl more. Have the man sell the action figure to the action figure buyer.

Finally he had enough. He went to his neighbor and bought the land. Have the man buy the field from his neighbor and hand him all the play money.

Then he dug up the pearl. He was so happy. Have the man dig up the pearl and act happy.

You may be wondering why he would give up everything for that pearl. That pearl was so valuable that he was able to sell it. Have the man sell the pearl to the pearl buyer and get all of the play money back.

He bought back the action figures. Have the man buy the action figures back.

He bought a better computer, a touch screen Apple, a 6S iPhone, the latest iPad, and a top of the art entertainment system. Have the man buy back the IPhone.

His wife was happy because he not only bought back her jewelry, he bought her a brand new diamond necklace. Have the man buy back the jewelry.

Then he bought a mansion to replace his house and furnished it with the best furniture. Have the man buy back the Lego house.

The actors can go back to their seats at this point.

Once he had the pearl of great price, everything else was available to him. That's the way it is with the Kingdom of God. When we seek Him first and make Him the foundation of our lives, everything else falls into place.

Praise and Worship

Object Lessons:

1. Fill the Jar

Supplies needed: canning jar or large glass jar with lid or a large round Rubbermaid container, large rocks, pebbles, sand

Preparation: Do this in advance to make sure everything fits and to determine how much of each item you need. Fill the jar first with the rocks, then with the pebbles, then with the sand. Make sure you can close the lid.

Place the sand in the jar. Ask the children if there's room for the rocks in the jar. Try to fit them in and show there's no way everything can fit and still close the lid.

These rocks represent Jesus. This is how some children try to serve God. They fit everything else into their lives first then, if there's room, they fit Jesus in. They're not building the right foundation.

Watch what happens when I put Jesus first.

Place the rocks in first. Ask the children if the jar is full. Pour in the pebbles. Talk about how these represent family, school, and other important things in life. Ask the children if the jar is full. Then pour in sand. Talk about how the sand could represent fun activities, video games, etc. Place the lid on the jar.

When we seek Jesus first, everything else fits.

2. Finding God

Supplies needed: binoculars, magnifying glass, Bible

When Jesus said today's memory verse, He first talked about all the things we need in our lives. I'll read the whole passage.

Read Matthew 6:25-33

If we seek after God first, He will meet our needs. Let me give an example of how to seek God.

Show items.

If I wanted to seek something far away, which of these items would I use? Binoculars

If I wanted to seek something very small, which item would I use? Magnifying glass

If I want to seek after God and His Kingdom which item would I use? Bible

That's right. When I want to seek after God, I will spend time with Him and get to know Him better. That means I'll spend time reading and learning about the Bible. I'll talk to Him with prayer. I'll want to be in His presence, so I'll spend time in praise and worship. And I'll want to be with His family, so I'll come to church often and spend time with other Christians. I'll do whatever I can to be in the presence of God.

I don't do these things 24 hours a day. I have other things I have to do. I need sleep, and I have to work to make money for a house and food. I also need to spend time with my family and take care of day to day activities. I even need to spend time relaxing and having fun, but if I really want to seek God first, I will make it my number 1 priority to do the things that help me spend time with God first.

Spending time with God is more important than any of these other activities. When God comes first, everything else will fall into place.

Optional Object Lesson: Investing in What Lasts

Supplies Needed: play money, video game or movie DVD, iPhone, football or sports item, glamor magazine or picture of a movie star, math or science book

Whatever you seek most is where your treasure is. It is the foundation your life is built upon.

Some people seek money and things they can buy. A century ago, in the 1920s, many people spent their time getting rich. They invested all of their money in the stock market or saved it in the bank for their future. Then something called the Great Depression happened in 1929. Banks closed and the stock market crashed. Many people who were rich lost everything. Those who put riches first in their lives had nothing left. They found out money is not a good foundation.

Some people seek entertainment and pleasure. They do whatever makes them feel good, but pleasure doesn't last. Those who build their life on entertainment are always looking for something else because nothing lasts.

Some people seek friendships. They are the ones who always want to be popular in school, but friends aren't perfect. Sometimes they disappoint us. Very few people still are friends with their childhood friends. Friendships don't last.

Some people are really into sports. They want to be great sports figures when they grow up. They work very hard at being good at sports. But even if they do make it in professional sports, if they've built the foundation of their lives on sports, they'll be disappointed. Most football players are retired by the age of 35 because of injuries or because they can't play as good as they did when they were younger. Sports don't last.

Some people want to be famous. They want to become movie stars or be in the next viral YouTube video. But even the most famous eventually lose some of their fame as they get older. People in Hollywood who have built their lives on being famous are unhappy.

Some people even try to build their lives on education. They study and learn as much as they can and get good grades. Then they go to college and grad school and graduate with honors. But some of these people can't find good jobs. Their education didn't help them in the long run. Even those who have good jobs, will eventually retire or die and find out that they built their lives on the wrong things.

None of the things I mentioned are wrong. Those who seek God first can have fun or make money or be into sports. They can have friends, be famous, and learn things. But if your treasure is in anything other than God, it won't last. That's why God tells us to build our lives on Him. He is our foundation. If we seek God first, everything else will fall into place.

Message: Righteousness, Peace, and Joy

Jesus is the foundation of the Kingdom of God. We have a good fountain in our lives when we seek him first. We can seek God by getting to know Him better through God's Word and through prayer, but we

also seek God when we spend time in His presence. In a moment we're going to do that, but first I want to tell you a few of the benefits of seeking God.

Romans 14:7 says "For the kingdom of God is not eating and drinking, but righteousness and peace and joy in the Holy Spirit." (NKJV)

This verse says the Kingdom of God is about our day to day lives. It's much bigger than that. When we put Jesus first in our lives, we build a foundation where God can fill us to overflowing in a way that affects every area of our daily lives.

Righteousness: *The first thing God wants to fill us with is His righteousness. When we put God first and spend time in His presence, He shows us the right thing to do, and He gives us the desire and power to do it. It may be hard to clean your room when your parents tell you too, but when you spend time in the presence of God, you will want to do what's right. You'll want to obey your parents. You could play praise music while you cleaning your room, and you might want to do the dishes too or help your parents out in other ways. When God fills you with righteousness, it becomes easier to do the right thing.*

Peace: *The next thing God wants to fill us with is peace. When we spend time in the presence of God and keep our focus on Him, He will fill us with supernatural peace. That peace isn't only for when things are going right. God will fill us with peace in the middle of when things are going wrong. That means you can have peace when you are being made fun of for being a Christian. You can have peace when you don't understand how to do a subject at school. You can have peace when your parents are arguing. No matter what is going on around you, God wants to fill you with His peace.*

Joy: *Another thing God wants to fill you with is His joy. God wants you to be happy, but He wants you to find that happiness through Him. When you spend time in God's presence, you might find yourself so happy you want to laugh. That's okay, because that means God is filling you with His joy. When He fills you with joy, all the stress and worry you have will go away. If you are depressed, God will deliver you from that depression with His joy. When we are satisfied in God, He fills us with His joy.*

Holy Spirit: *God also wants to fill you with His Holy Spirit. When you are filled with the Holy Spirit and speak in tongues, God will give you supernatural power. This might mean you will pray for someone to be healed, and he is healed. You might hear God speaking a word to you that you are supposed to tell someone. There are a lot of other ways God can give you power. One power you will receive is the power to be His witnesses. That means you'll have the power to tell other people about God.*

Response Time: Leaders, make sure you are prepared for a move of God in this service. Have somebody other than you to guide the children when needed or to catch them if they are slain in the Spirit. Be careful not to orchestrate what happens. Let God take charge. Have worship music prepared to play on a loop. During worship time, if I child is overcome, lay your hand gently on his or her head and wait until you know you are supposed to go on. God will use you. After the response time, give children an opportunity to testify about what happened to them. Also ask the children if God spoke anything to them during this time. Refrain from reacting negatively to their testimonies even if you have to guide them doctrinally. Once you've introduced the children to worshipping and seeking God, arrange response time in this way every week. Children will want to spend time in the presence of God.

God wants you to seek Him so you can be filled with all of these wonderful gifts. During response time, we are going to put on some worship music. I want you all to close your eyes, raise your hands, and focus on God. You can sing, or you can praise Him with your words. The important thing is to seek His presence.

While you are doing this, some things might happen that have never happened before. You might be so overcome by the Holy Spirit that you can't stand up. If that happens, you can sit or lie on the floor. If you fall back, somebody will be there to catch you. You might be filled with so much peace that you just stand there, or you kneel, or you cry. That's okay. Some of you may be filled with joy to the point where you laugh hysterically. That's okay too. Some of you will find your mouth trying to form words that are confusing. If that happens, stop speaking English and speak out what God is speaking through you. That is the Baptism of the Holy Spirit.

Small Group Chat: Treasure Hunt

Supplies Needed: small objects hidden around the room.

For this small group chat, give children a list of small objects hidden around the room. Give them a time limit for finding the objects. You can have them work as a team trying to beat the clock. When the game is over, ask the following questions.

Treasure hunters love to search for valuable objects. Some of them say the search is as fun as finding the treasure. Was it fun searching for these objects?

Jesus is the greatest treasure of all. He tells us in Matthew 6:33 to seek Him first. What are some of the ways we can do that?

The Journey: City on a Hill, Lesson 2

City on a Hill Lesson 2: The Wise Builder

Focus Point: God wants us to obey Him, so we can be wise.

Goal: Children will learn when they build their lives on Jesus and obey Him, they are being wise. When they reject Jesus or disobey His word, they are being foolish.

Memory Verse: Matthew 7:24 *Therefore everyone who hears these words of mine and puts them into practice is like a wise man who built his house on the rock.*

Supplies Needed:

- *The Journey* Videos (free with registration)
- *The Journey* Jpeg Slides (free with registration)
- Copies of *The Journey* Family Devotional Sheet (free with registration)
- Road Construction Costume: hardhat, yellow or orange caution vest, walkie-talkie
- police puppet or costume
- Index cards
- 2 cookie sheets or trays
- 2 small Lego block houses (could use paper cups with houses drawn on them)
- Sand
- Big rock
- Pitcher of water
- Instructions for building a birdhouse (You can print these out on the internet.)
- Bible
- Optional Small Group Activity: Supplies needed to build a birdhouse or popsicle sticks

Opening: *The Journey Countdown* or *City on a Hill* or *The Journey* Intro Slide (Available free with registration of this curriculum.)

Welcome: Welcome the children and tell them how excited you to see them. Today we are going to learn to be wise builders.

Prayer: Ask a child to pray over the service.

Rules: (use rules slide)

Go over the *5 Ups Rules*: 1. Sit up straight. 2. Listen up. 3. Hush up. 4. Don't get up and run around or go to the bathroom. 5. Worship Up! (stand and participate during praise and worship)

Theme or Activity Songs: Choose one or two fast moving activity songs that goes with the curriculum.

Memory Verse Skit: Listen to the Police (use *City on a Hill* lesson 2, slide A)

Supplies needed: police officer puppet or uniform

Peace Officer Shalom: Hi boys and girls. I'm Police Officer Shalom. They call me that because I keep the peace by arresting wrong doers, but I also protect the community. Sometimes people don't want to listen to police officers. They feel like they know better than the police officers what they should do. We police officers are there to protect and serve. We have a dangerous job, and it is important to do what a police officer says even if disagree with him.

For instance, one time I told a teenager not to go into the woods. The teenager told me the woods were public property, and he could do whatever he wanted. What he didn't know was a very bad man had run into the woods earlier, and the police officers were surrounding the woods waiting for him to come out. I was trying to protect the teenager and my fellow police officers.

The teenager ran into the woods, and I had to endanger myself to run in after him. The bad man shot at us, and I was shot in the leg. Nobody would have been hurt if that teenager would have listened to me. After two more police officers apprehended the subject and got me medical attention, they arrested the teenager.

It's wise to listen to a police officer. We also need to listen to God and obey Him because He knows what is best. Today's memory verse is Matthew 7:24. "Therefore everyone who hears these words of mine and puts them into practice is like a wise man who built his house on the rock." Be wise by listening to and obeying God.

Game Time: Follow the Leader (use game time slide)

One child is chosen to be it and leaves the room with an assistant. Another child is chosen to be the leader. The children all stand in a circle and the child who is it is in the middle. The leader makes motions and does activities and everyone in the circle does everything the leader does. The children in the circle should be cautioned not to make it obvious who the leader is. The child who is it tries to guess who the leader is. Once he guesses, the leader is it and the game starts again.

A lot of people follow the wrong leaders in life. A wise person will follow Jesus Christ as his leader.

Offering: *Jesus said that it's better to give than to receive. If I want to build my life on Jesus, then I will want to give. Giving includes a lot of things. We can give to the poor. We can give to our friends. We can also give in offerings. That's why we receive offerings every week, to give you an opportunity to give.*

This might also be a good opportunity to give canned goods to a benevolence project in your church or collect blankets and toiletries for homeless people.

Skit: The Wise Builder

Supplies needed: Road Guy costume, walkie-talkie

Ralph: (Wanders in wearing a tool belt.)

Leader: Hi Ralph, how's the building project going?

Ralph: Not good. We've had a few setbacks. Now we're behind schedule.

Leader: What kind of setbacks?

Ralph: The boss hired a new man, a cousin of the mayor. He doesn't know anything about construction.

Leader: I could see how that could slow things down. Did you try to teach him what to do?

Ralph: I tried, but it didn't work.

Leader: What happened?

Ralph: It's like this. That new man won't listen to anything we say, and he won't follow the blueprints. I showed him on the blueprints where we needed eight steel beams that were 12 feet long. He tried to use wood beams.

Leader: Wow, steel beams are stronger than wood beams. They're important to have in a sky-scraper.

Ralph: Not only that, but he cut the wood beams different lengths. Some of them were only 11 feet, 11 inches, and some of them were 12 feet, one inch.

Leader: That would make the floor he was working on lopsided.

Ralph: You've got that right, but it gets even worse.

Leader: What could be worse than that?

Ralph: He got tired of cutting those beams, so he only used six beams instead of eight.

Leader: Oh no. Doesn't he know that if he doesn't have enough beams, the whole floor might come down?

Ralph: He does now 'cause that's just what happened. The floor caved in. The bad part was nobody knew what he did. They'd built two floors above his. All three floors collapsed, and they *damaged the floor below. We had to tear out four floors and redo them. The boss was really mad.*

Leader: What happened when the boss found out about the wood beams.

Ralph: He fired the new man. He said he didn't care whose cousin he is. He needs wise builders who follow instructions not foolish builders who don't do as their told.

Leader: That could apply to what we're learning today. The Bible says that when we listen to what God says, we are wise builders who build our lives upon the rock. The rock is Jesus Christ.

Ralph: What does the Bible say about foolish builders like the guy the boss just fired?

Leader: Foolish builders are those who don't obey God. They are like a man who builds his house on the sand. When the storm comes, the house is swept away.

Ralph: Kind of like those four floors of the sky-scraper were swept away.

Leader: Exactly.

Ralph: Well, I need to go now. We all have to work overtime to rebuild those four floors. Bye. (Ralph exits.)

Memory Verse: Matthew 7:24 *Therefore everyone who hears these words of mine and puts them into practice is like a wise man who built his house on the rock.*

Memory Verse Talk: (use *City on a Hill* lesson 2, slide A)

Following instructions when we want to build things is important, but building our lives on Jesus, the solid rock, is even more important. One way we do that is by following what God says to do.

Memory Verse Activity: Crazy Voices

Supplies needed: index cards

Preparation: Write different kinds of crazy voice on index cards. Examples might be a frog, a mouse, a cheerleader, a British Accent, a football player, a cowboy, a Southerner, a New Yorker, etc.

Place each word of the verse on a separate piece of paper. If you have a smaller ministry, make enough cards for every child. If you have a larger ministry, make 10 cards.

Have each child participating, choose a card at random. Each child with a card quotes the memory verse using the crazy voice on the card. The other children guess which kind of voice it is.

When we listen to God's Word and the Spirit of God inside of us, we are like the wise builder who built his house upon a rock.

Bible Story: The Foolish Man and the Wise Man (Matthew 7:24-27)

Read the Bible Story from the Bible in an easy to understand version.

Ask the children what things people build their lives on that will wash away during the storms of life. Some answers might be friends, money, things, sports, etc.

Ask the children about how they can build their lives on the rock, Jesus Christ. If they need help answering this question, offer suggestions such as obeying God, spending time with God, worshipping, reading the Bible, praying.

Video: House on the Sand (*City on a Hill* videos available upon registration of materials)

Praise and Worship

Object Lessons:

1. Building on the Right Foundation

Supplies needed: 2 cookie sheets or trays, two small Lego block houses (could use paper cups with houses drawn on them), sand, big rock, pitcher of water

Preparations: Pour a sand hill on one tray and place the house on it. Place the rock on the other tray and place the house on it. It would be a good idea to do this ahead of time to make sure it works right.

Storms come into everyone's life. There's no way to avoid bad things happening. What are some of the storms that happen in kid's lives? Have children answer. Some suggestions are divorce, bullying, bad grades, health issues, etc.

We can't avoid these storms, but we can be prepared for them. This is what happens when the storms come to someone who doesn't build his life on Jesus. Pour water on tray with the sand. The house should be swept away with the sand.

If we build our lives on Jesus and seek Him first, we have a solid foundation to help us weather storms. Pour water on the tray with the rock. Don't pour directly on the house. The house should remain standing along with the rock.

2. Follow the Instructions

Supplies needed: Instructions for building a birdhouse (You can print these out on the internet.), Bible

Read the instructions part way through, then stop and act frustrated.

I was going to build a birdhouse, but these instructions are too complicated. I've decided to just wing it. I don't need the instructions.

What do you think would happen if I decided to build a birdhouse that way? Let the children answer.

If I built a birdhouse without the instructions, it would be a mess. If I want it to turn out all right, I will follow the instructions. Following the instructions makes me a wise builder. That's true with my life to, but being a wise builder when it comes to our lives is much more important than when building a birdhouse. I want to be a wise builder, so I'm going to read and follow the instructions. Hold up your Bible. *This has the instructions for life. In this book is what God wants to tell me about how to live my life. When I build my life on Jesus, I will obey the instructions in this book. Jesus said that makes me a wise life builder.*

Message: The Wise Christian

We've been talking about how a wise person builds his life on Jesus. Now I'm going to tell you how to do that.

First, start a relationship with Jesus. If you aren't saved, if you haven't given your life to Jesus and made Him your Lord and Savior, you can't be good enough to be a wise life builder. That kind of wisdom comes from God.

Once we accept Jesus as our Lord, we need to do what He says. John 14:5 says, "If you love me, keep my commandments." You can't love God enough to keep His commandments unless you are His child.

Second, ask God to forgive you and cleanse you whenever you do something wrong like King David did when he sinned. 1 John 1:9 says, "If we confess our sins, he is faithful and just to forgive us our sins and to cleanse us from all unrighteousness." A wise Christian confesses His sins to God.

Third, follow God's instructions. If we want to know what God wants us to do, we can find out by reading the Bible and by praying and asking God. God wants to tell you how to live a life built on Him so that you can make wise choices like King David.

The last thing is to walk in the Spirit. God puts the Holy Spirit in each one of us when we are saved, but we have to cooperate with the Holy Spirit. Listen to God's voice when He nudges you to do something and then do it. The more you spend time in the presence of God, the easier it becomes to walk in the Spirit.

For response time, pray for the children who come forward for salvation and wisdom on how to walk in the Spirit. Then play worship music and lead children into the presence of God. Make sure to take time before worship time to give instructions. After the response time, ask the children if God has spoken anything to them. If the answer is yes, let the children speak what they heard. Talk about how it is important to listen to God's voice and obey it.

Small Group Project: The Birdhouse

You can discuss the lesson with the small groups, or you can follow the instructions for the birdhouse from the object lesson earlier in the lesson and have the children work as a group to build a birdhouse. If you are not good at carpentry, have a few men from the church who know how to build a birdhouse and have the supplies and tools to help you. Or you can buy kits to build houses or bird houses.

Another idea is to have the children build houses out of Popsicle sticks and decorate them.

City on a Hill Lesson 3 – Jesus, the Master Builder

Focus Point: We surrender our lives so God can build us into his spiritual house.

Goal: Students will learn that Jesus is the master builders, but they need to surrender their lives to Him so that He can build their lives the way He wants to.

Memory Verse: 1 Peter 2:5a *You also, like living stones, are being built into a spiritual house…*

Supplies Needed:

- *The Journey* Videos (free with registration)
- *The Journey* Jpeg Slides (free with registration)
- Copies of *The Journey* Family Devotional Sheet (free with registration)
- Road Construction Costume: hardhat, yellow or orange caution vest, walkie-talkie
- police puppet or costume
- Colored post-it notes or pieces of construction paper
- Blindfolds
- 2 sets of papers with one word of the memory verse on each paper
- Lesson 3 Images 1 and 2 (free with registration)

Opening: *The Journey Countdown* or *City on a Hill* or *The Journey* Intro Slide

Welcome: Welcome the children and tell them how excited you to see them. Review the last 2 weeks.

Prayer: Ask a child to pray over the service.

Rules: (use rules slide)

Go over the *5 Ups Rules*: 1. Sit up straight. 2. Listen up. 3. Hush up. 4. Don't get up and run around or go to the bathroom. 5. Worship Up! (stand and participate during praise and worship)

Theme or Activity Songs: Choose one or two fast moving activity songs that goes with the curriculum.

Memory Verse Skit: Surrender (use *City on a Hill* lesson 3, slide A)

Supplies needed: police officer puppet or uniform

Peace Officer Shalom: Hi boys and girls. I'm Police Officer Shalom. They call me that because I keep the peace by arresting wrong doers. One of the biggest problems I have in being a police officer is that wrong doers don't want to surrender. It happens in all situations, and it makes my life more dangerous. Sometimes it put other people in danger as well.

Let me give you an example. I clocked someone going 60 miles per hour in a school zone. I was worried he might endanger children on their way to school and immediately turned my lights and siren on. At this point, the driver was supposed to surrender and pull to the side of the road so that I could give him a ticket. Instead, he decided to take off. He ran a red light and two stops signs before we caught up with him, but the worst part is he almost hit a child with his car. Fortunately, the child is going to be okay.

I try not to get angry, but I was angry at that driver. He put everyone in danger and almost killed a child because he didn't want to surrender to the proper authorities and get the ticket he deserved. Instead of getting a ticket, he's now in jail.

In the same way that people should surrender to police officers, God wants us to surrender to Him in all areas of our lives. God is building us into spiritual living houses to share the Gospel, but if we don't surrender every room of our house to Him, we limit how He can work in our lives. Our memory verse today is 1 Peter 2:5a. "You also, like living stones, are being built into a spiritual house…" I have to go now. I have more wrong doers to catch so that I can make the street safe. Good-bye.

Game Time: Mine Fields (use game time slide)

Supplies needed: Colored post-it notes or pieces of construction paper, blindfolds

Preparation: Set colored pieces of paper in various places on the path you want the kids to take. This game consists of teams of two. You can have as many teams as you want, but you'll need one blindfold for each team.

One partner of each team is blindfolded and start at a different place at the beginning of the path. They must walk through a "mine field" made up of the pieces of paper without stepping on any mines. The other partner stands to the side and tells the blind-folded partner where to walk to get to the other side. He must listen carefully for his partner because each partner is giving different directions. If he touches a mine, he's out.

There are many landmines in the Christian life. There are distractions that want to keep you from God's will. There are also obstacles and sins. If you follow God's direction to get through these landmines instead of going your own way, you'll be safe. Jesus is the master builder. He knows where the landmines are and how to get you around them.

Offering: *If we want God to build our lives according to His plans, we surrender our lives to Him. That includes our money. We don't need to give all of our money in the offering at church, but we do recognize that our money is God's money that He is allowing us to use.*

Skit: Building a City

Supplies needed: Road Guy costume, walkie-talkie

Ralph: (Wanders in wearing a tool belt mumbling to himself) If that don't beat all. I tell you.

Leader: Hello, Ralph. What's the matter?

Ralph: What makes you think something's wrong?

Leader: For one thing, you're mumbling to yourself. For another, you keep saying "if that don't beat all."

Ralph: I guess you're right. There is something wrong.

Leader: Do you want to tell us about it?

Ralph: I guess. It won't do any good, but I would like to get it off my chest. You know how I'm working on the city project to build sky scrapers downtown?

Leader: I sure do. You've been talking about it for weeks.

Ralph: It looks like we might not be able to finish the job. What makes it worse is all the construction workers might be laid off, so I might be out of a job again.

Leader: I'm so sorry, Ralph. Why might the job be cancelled?

Ralph: It's like this. Before the city decided to revitalize downtown, the city planner went to all the home owners and made an agreement to buy their houses at a fair price. Well, today, one of the residents changed her mind.

Leader: I can't see how one person could hold up building a whole city.

Ralph: Normally she couldn't, but her house is smack dab in the middle of the building project. If she doesn't change her mind, we'll have to stop the work on building the city.

Leader: Can she do that?

Ralph: She sure can. She hasn't signed the papers yet even though she agreed to the deal, and now she's holding out for more money. If she doesn't agree to surrender her house for the sum she agreed to, I'll be out of a job, and the city will be out of a lot of money for land they can't use.

Leader: That sort of reminds me of our lesson today. God wants to build us into spiritual houses that reflect His glory, but if we don't surrender everything to Him, we stop Him from building us into what He wants us to be.

Ralph: Do you mean you can't hold anything back from God?

Leader: Nothing. We need to surrender our minds, our hearts, our hands, eyes, and ears to God for him to make us into the spiritual houses He wants us to be.

Ralph: It does sound a little like this city project. Unless every single person sells their house to the city, we can't do anymore building.

Leader: Just like God can't build our lives around Him unless we surrender everything.

Ralph: Maybe the city can be saved. I have an idea. I have to go now. I'll tell you how it all works out. (Exits)

Memory Verse: 1 Peter 2:5a *You also, like living stones, are being built into a spiritual house…*

Memory Verse Talk: (use *The Bible, Your GPS for Life* lesson 3, slide A)

Today we're talking about how God is the master builder of our lives. The parts of our lives are like living stones. God wants to take those parts and build them.

Memory Verse Activity: Building a House

Supplies Needed: Two copies of Lesson 3 Image 1. Two copies of Lesson 3 Image 2. To make the contest harder, have sheets of papers in each set with random words on them. Image 2 shows what the house should look like when it is done.

Preparation: Cut out and copy the squares with words in them in Lesson 3 Image 2. You'll want two sets Tape the copies Lesson 3 Image 1 on the wall or a marker board. Mix up both sets of the words from Image 2 and throw them in two piles. Divide the children into two teams. The first team to build the house by arranging the words of the verse wins.

Bible Story: The Rich Young Ruler (Mark 10:17-22)

Supplies Needed: A bag of play money or gold coin wrapped chocolates

Set the bag of money aside as you tell the story of the rich young ruler in your own words.

Once a man who was very rich came to Jesus and asked "what must I do to have eternal life?" This man had heard Jesus was in the area, and he wanted to serve Jesus. He was a good man who did good things. Jesus told him to obey the commandments. This rich young ruler told Jesus that he had followed the commandments since he was young. Jesus then told him to go and sell everything he had, and he would have treasure in Heaven.

Pick up the bag of fake money. *Jesus didn't tell him this because you have to get rid of everything to serve Him. Jesus knew the rich young ruler loved his money more than he loved God. He wasn't willing to surrender his money to God. The young man went away very sad. Jesus couldn't be his master builder because he wouldn't surrender his money.*

Hold up the bag of fake money. *If there anything in your life that is more important to you than God? Is there anything that would be hard to give up if God asked you to? If we want Jesus to build our lives, we have to be willing to surrender everything to him. Don't be like the rich young ruler who went away sad.*

Praise and Worship

Object Lessons: Rooms in My House

1. **Jesus the Master Builder of My House** (use *City on a Hill* lesson 3, slides A-B)

   Let's review our memory verse for today one more time. 1 Peter 2:5a "You also, like living stones, are being built into a spiritual house…"

Jesus is our master builder. He is the only one who can build our lives into something that honors Him. He has a purpose for each and every one of us.

The word built here means to furnish, equip, prepare, make ready; of one who makes ready for a person or thing; of builders, to construct, erect, with the included idea of adorning and equipping with all things necessary.

The choice is ours. Jesus can only build our lives if we surrender every room to Him. He knows how to build our lives because He had the blueprints before we were ever born.

2. I Surrender My Heart

(use *City on a Hill* lesson 3, slide C)

Proverbs 4:23 says "Above all else, guard your heart, for everything you do flows from it."

Someone once said that the kitchen is the heart of the home. This is because, in the kitchen, meals are prepared to keep us healthy. When I was young, families would eat together in the kitchen. This was when they would talk about their day and catch up with each other. Sometimes we would play board games or cards together in the kitchen. When company came over we would sit around the table and talk after we ate together.

Jesus wants to be Lord of the kitchen in your life. He wants you to give your life to Him. We do that when we get saved. We ask Jesus to come into our hearts and forgive us of our sin. When we do that, He gives us a new heart. He becomes the master builder of our hearts.

3. I Surrender My Mind

(use lesson 3, *City on a Hill* slide D)

Romans 12:2 Do not conform to the pattern of this world, but be transformed by the renewing of your mind. Then you will be able to test and approve what God's will is--his good, pleasing and perfect will.

Your bedroom is a secret place, a place of peace. It's where you sleep and dream and where you get ready for your day every morning. Some children have all their toys and prize possessions in their bedrooms. The bedroom is an important place.

Our minds are like our bedrooms. Our thoughts and emotions are where we keep our prize possessions. It's where we dream and get ready to live our lives. When we keep our minds on God, He promises to give us peace.

Sometimes we have to renew our minds. We can't let our minds think about worldly things like being angry with someone and thinking about ways to get even or thinking about things that go against God's Word.

Jesus wants us to surrender our minds to Him. He will create a bedroom in our lives that prepares us to serve Him.

4. I Surrender My Hands (use *City on a Hill* lesson 3, Slide E)

Some homes have offices where people work on their computers or workrooms where they build things. In these rooms, people work with their hands. They do things. What we do should reflect that Jesus is our master builder. That's why we need to surrender our hands or our offices to Him. We show the world that we have surrendered our lives to God by what we do. If we do bad things all the time like stealing, lying, cheating, or being mean, we show that Jesus isn't really the master builder of our lives. If we do good things like being kind even when people are mean to us, or not going along with our friends when they want to do something wrong, or even not cleaning our rooms or doing our homework when our parents tell us to, we're showing that we really haven't surrendered our hands or the office of our lives to Jesus.

Jesus wants us to surrender our hands to Him so He can help us do things that please Him.

5. I Surrender My Eyes and Ears (use *City on a Hill* lesson 3, Slide F)

Luke 11:34(ICB) Your eye is a light for the body. If your eyes are good, then your whole body will be full of light. But if your eyes are evil, then your whole body will be full of darkness.

A lot of things come into our eyes and ears when we are in the living room or recreation room. That's where people watch television, listen to music, play video games, and read. There's nothing wrong with entertainment. God wants us to enjoy ourselves, but we need to surrender our entertainment to God. If we want Jesus to be the master builder of the living area of our lives, we need to make sure we don't watch TV, play video games, listen to music, or read books that go against God.

Jesus wants to be the master builder of what goes in our eyes and ears so He can build a living area that honors Him.

Message: I Surrender All

I want you to examine your house. Have you given Jesus every area of your lives?

Kitchen: Have you given your heart to Him and become born again? If not, with nobody looking around raise your hands, and I'll lead you in a prayer of salvation. Lead the children in a prayer of salvation.

Bedroom: Have you surrendered your thoughts to Christ? Do you need to renew your mind?

Office or Workroom: Do you show that Jesus is your master builder by the things you do, or do you need to work on that area?

Living Room: Are you allowing entertainment into your eyes and ears that doesn't please God?

There's one more area you need to surrender if you want to surrender everything to God. That's your hidden places, your closets. The sin nobody knows about. Ask God if you have sin in your life you need to get rid of.

Play worship music while you lead the response time. You may want to instruct the children to kneel and close their eyes so God can show them areas they need to surrender to Him. Pray for each child.

Small Group Chat: Jesus, Our Master Builder

Ask these question as discussion starters.

What are some things we should be thinking if we've surrendered to Jesus is our master builder?

What are some things we shouldn't be thinking?

What are some things that show Jesus is our master builder?

What things show we haven't surrendered everything to Jesus?

What kind of entertainment is okay for someone who has surrendered his life to Christ?

What kind of entertainment is not okay?

City on a Hill Lesson 4 – A Shining City on a Hill

Focus Point: Christ wants us to live for Him.

Goal: Students will learn that when they build their lives on Jesus, they show Jesus in everything they do and say.

Memory Verse: Matthew 5:16 *In the same way, let your light shine before others, that they may see your good deeds and glorify your Father in heaven.*

Supplies Needed:

- *The Journey* Videos (free with registration)
- *The Journey* Jpeg Slides (free with registration)
- Copies of *The Journey* Family Devotional Sheet (free with registration)
- Road Construction Costume: hardhat, yellow or orange caution vest, walkie-talkie
- police puppet or costume
- Flashlight
- Basket
- Oil lamp
- Oil
- Optional Science Experiment: black tissue paper or cloth, Styrofoam ball, cooking skewer or small wooden dowel rod, flashlight
- Optional Small Group Craft: empty paper towel or toilet paper rolls, small paper plates, yellow tissue paper, markers and stickers ect. to decorate

Opening: *The Journey Countdown* or *City on a Hill* or *The Journey* Intro Slide (Available free with registration of this curriculum.)

Welcome: Welcome the children and tell them how excited you to see them. Talk about how this is the last week for teaching about A City on a Hill. *We are that city so we can live our lives for Jesus. The first week, we learned that we need to build our lives on the only firm foundation, Jesus. The second week, we learned that a wise builder builds his life on the solid rock by obeying God's Word. Last week, we learned that Jesus is the master builder. When we surrender out lives to Him, He will build us into what He wants us to be. This week, we're learning that God wants us to be a city on a hill so others will see our lives as a shining light that points people to Jesus.*

Prayer: Ask a child to pray over the service.

Rules: (use rules slide)

Go over the *5 Ups Rules*: 1. Sit up straight. 2. Listen up. 3. Hush up. 4. Don't get up and run around or go to the bathroom. 5. Worship Up! (stand and participate during praise and worship)

Theme or Activity Songs: Choose one or two fast moving activity songs that goes with the curriculum.

Memory Verse Skit: Traffic Lights (use *City on a Hill* lesson 4, slide A)

Supplies needed: police officer puppet or uniform

Peace Officer Shalom: Hi boys and girls. I'm Police Officer Shalom. They call me that because I keep the peace by making sure people are safe. One of the greatest inventions to keep people safe in their cars is the traffic light. Stop signs are great for roads that aren't used as often, but when there is a busy street, a traffic light saves lives.

When a car comes to a traffic light, the color the light is shining tells the driver what to do. If the light is green, it's safe to go. If the light is yellow, the driver should use caution. If the light is red, the driver should stop. If the driver doesn't stop, there might be a wreck. People could get hurt.

God puts traffic lights in our lives through God's Word and the prompting of the Holy Spirit. He wants us to let our lives shine for Him. That means when God's Word tells us what to do, we should go and do it. When the Holy Spirit warns us to be cautious, we should listen. And when something goes against God's Word or the prompting of the Holy Spirit, we should immediately stop. This is one way we let our lights shine.

Our memory verse today is Matthew 5:16. "In the same way, let your light shine before others, that they may see your good deeds and glorify your Father in heaven." I have to go on traffic patrol now. I've enjoyed taking this journey with you.

Game Time: Red Light Green Light (use game time slide)

In this game, one person plays the "stop light" and the rest try to touch him/her.

At the start, all the children form a line about 15 feet away from the stop light.

The stop light faces away from the line of kids and says "green light". At this point the kids are allowed to move towards the stoplight.

At any point, the stop light may say "red light!" and turn around. If any of the kids are caught moving after this has occurred, they are out.

Play resumes when the stop light turns back around and says "green light".

The stop light wins if all the kids are out before anyone is able to touch him/her. Otherwise, the first player to touch the stop light wins the game and earns the right to be "stop light" for the next game.

Just as in this game, we go when green light is called and stop when red light is called, we should always listen to God's Word and the Holy Spirit to let our lives shine. This way we'll go when God wants us to and stop when God wants us to.

The Journey: City on a Hill, Lesson 4

Offering: This would be a good opportunity to take an offering for missions. Tell the children a story about a missionary your church is supporting who is letting His light shine in a foreign land for Jesus. End the story with talking about how we can help the missionary let his light shine by giving to missions in the offering.

Skit: A Shining City

Supplies needed: Road Guy costume, walkie-talkie

Ralph: I'm so excited. We're almost done building the city on a hill.

Leader: That's awesome, Ralph. I thought you couldn't finish because of that woman who changed her mind about selling her house.

Ralph: The city planners met with the woman, and she realized it was wrong to promise to sell and change her mind.

Leader: That's great. When will you be done with the buildings?

Ralph: We have the buildings all built and the tenants are ready to move in.

Leader: I thought you said you were almost done. If you have everything already built, what do you have left to do?

Ralph: We have to put in the electricity and the street lights. Without light, the buildings aren't done.

Leader: I didn't think about that. The city you built on the hill would be dark without electricity and street lights.

Ralph: That's right. We are going to light up all the buildings so people can see them from miles. Then we'll put in lots of street lights so people can find their way around the city.

Leader: That's a good idea. Today's our last day learning about how God wants to build our lives as a city on a hill. Today we're talking about letting our lights shine for God.

Ralph: That's even more important than lighting the city we're building. When we let our lights shine for God, we can share the love of Jesus with others.

Leader: That's right, Ralph. I have to admit I'm a little sad today is our last day with you.

Ralph: Maybe not. I've learned a lot about letting God build my life for Him, so I'm sure He'll let our paths cross again.

Leader: I'm sure He will. Thanks for all you've taught us about building a city.

Ralph: You're welcome. Good-bye, everyone.

Memory Verse: Matthew 5:16 *In the same way, let your light shine before others, that they may see your good deeds and glorify your Father in heaven.*

Memory Verse Talk: (use *City on a Hill* lesson 4, slide A)

Today's verse is about being a light for other people by letting our lights shine for God. We should live in such a way that people praise God because of the good things we do. When we do this, we are a city on a hill, shining for Jesus.

Memory Verse Activity: Quote the Verse If...

Have the children stand and quote the verse if they meet the criteria you announce. Some suggestions are *Quote the verse if*:

You brushed your teeth today.

You ate breakfast.

You have brown eyes.

You have red hair.

Continue until every child has had a chance to quote the verse.

Object Lessons:

1. Lights Out

Supplies needed: flashlight, basket

Have any of you ever been at home at night when the lights went out? I have too. Sometimes this happens because of a storm, and sometimes a transformer that supplies energy goes out.

What does your family do when the lights go out? Let the children answer.

In my house, when the lights go out, I stumble around in the dark, and sometimes stub my toe until I find my flashlight. Turn on the flashlight. *Once I find my flashlight and turn it on, I can see where I'm going.*

In Matthew 5, Jesus tells us that Christians are like a city on a hill that shines bright and can't be hidden. My flashlight isn't that bright, but it does help me keep from running into things.

What if, when the lights go out, I turned on my flashlight then hid it under a basket. Place the flashlight under a basket. *That would be silly, wouldn't it? What good would a flashlight do if its light was hidden under a basket? You need to turn it on so that you can see. In the same way, let your light shine before others, that they may see your good deeds and glorify your Father in heaven.*

I don't know about you, but I plan to let my light shine.

2. Oil Lamp

Supplies needed: oil lamp, oil

In Bible days, people didn't have electricity or flashlights. Most of them didn't even have candles because it took too long to make them. People in the Bible days used oil lamps. Show the oil lamp and light it. *Their oil lamps looked different, but the principle is the same. The wick goes in the bowl of oil.* Show oil. *When you light the wick, the oil keeps the light burning bright. When the oil ran out, the light would go out.*

It's the same way with us. When we spend time with Jesus, our lights shine brightly for Him, but when we allow the oil to go out, then our lights will dim. We stop wanting to spend time with Jesus. We might stop reading our Bibles, going to church, praying, and worshiping. Our light comes from Jesus in our lives. When we are full of Jesus, we can let our light shine before others, that they may see our good deeds and glorify our Father in heaven.

Praise and Worship

Optional Science Experiment: Reflectors

Supplies needed: Black tissue paper or cloth, Styrofoam ball, cooking skewer or small wooden dowel rod, flashlight

Preparation: Tack black paper or cloth on the wall or a marker board. This helps to keep the light from bouncing back onto the ball from behind. Stick your skewer or dowel rod into your Styrofoam ball, aka the moon. Turn off any lights in the room and pull the shades for a greater effect. Try this out ahead of time to get an idea of how to shine the flashlight for the different phases.

Did you know the moon has no light at all? When you see moonlight, what you are really seeing is the sun reflecting off the moon.

To show the full moon, shine a flashlight, aka Sun, directly onto your moon.

As you can see, the moon doesn't have any light of its own. When we see the full moon, we're really seeing the sun shining directly on it, but what about when we see phases of the moon?

Move your Moon around the Sun a little to show another phase of the moon. *Notice how part of the Moon is now in shadow.* Continue moving the Moon around the Sun to show how the positioning causes part of the moon to be in shadow. *Here you can see the different phases of the moon depending on how directly the sun is shining.*

Move the flashlight behind the Styrofoam ball. *This is called a New Moon. The sun is barely reflected off the moon's surface.*

Shine the flashlight directly on the moon again. *As you can see by this experiment, the more the sun is reflecting on the moon, the brighter the moon shines. That's how we reflect the light of God in our lives. The closer we get to God and the more time we spend in His presence, the greater His light will shine in us.*

Bible Story: Turning the World Upside Down (Acts 1-13; 17:6)

Supplies Needed: Instrumental music

Today's Bible story is about the early church in the book of Acts and how they let their light shine in such a way that they turned the world upside down. Tell this story in a dramatic way with powerful soundtrack music playing in the background.

In Acts 17:6, it was said about the early church, "These who have turned the world upside down have come here too." The reason the early church was able to do this was because they let God's light shine through them. They spent time in the presence of God, then they did what the Holy Spirit told them to do, and they followed what God said. Let's look at a few things that happened.

In Acts 2, on the day of Pentecost, the disciples were having a prayer meeting that lasted 10 days. They were praying and asking God for the Holy Spirit to lead them. Tongues of fire appeared, and the sound of a mighty wind blew. The disciples were baptized in the Holy Spirit and began to speak in unknown languages.

In Acts 4, Believers spoke God's Word without fear even though they were in danger, and 5,000 people were saved.

In Acts 5, the apostles did many signs and miracles

In Acts 6 & 7, Stephan did miracles, preached the Gospel, and forgave those who stoned him to death.

In Acts 8, Phillip was told by the Holy Spirit to go down a desert road. He listened and found an Ethiopian official there who was reading Scripture but didn't understand it. Phillip taught Him about Jesus. The Ethiopian got saved, and Phillip baptized him. Then Phillip was miraculously transported to another place by the Holy Spirit.

In Acts 9, Saul saw a light from Heaven when Jesus appeared. He surrendered his life to God and changed his name to Paul. He received his sight, had visions from God, preached to the world with boldness and wrote 2/3 New Testament.

Also in Acts 9, Peter healed people and raised someone from the dead.

In Acts 10, Roman Soldiers were baptized in the Holy Spirit and spoke in other tongues.

In Acts 12, Peter was rescued from prison by an angel.

In Acts 13, Barnabas and Paul become missionaries and shared the Gospel everywhere they went.

The entire book of Acts shows how the early church listened to God, did what He said, and how God shined His light through them so others would see the light of God. God is still doing that today through believers who love Him and follow Him. He wants to shine His light through you so other may see your good works and glorify God.

Message: Letting Our Lights Shine

How do we let our lights shine for Jesus?

Read John 8:12. *First we recognize that the light doesn't come from us. Like the moon reflects the sun, we only reflect God's light. So we need to be saved to reflect Jesus' light.*

The Bible is called a lamp unto our feet, so we need to spend time in God's Word and learn what it says so God's light will direct us.

Read 1 John 1:5-7. *We spend time in the presence of God. The more time we spend with God, the more we will reflect His light.*

For response time, play worship music and encourage your students to spend time in the presence of God. Afterwards, ask your students if any of them heard God tell them what they can do to shine God's light.

Small Group Chat: Let Your Light Shine Craft

Supplies Needed: empty paper towel or toilet paper rolls, small paper plates, yellow tissue paper, markers and stickers ect. to decorate

Have children decorate the paper towel rolls (candles). Have them stuff yellow tissue paper on top to look like a candle light. Have them glue the paper towel rolls on a small paper plate as a candle holder.

Would a candle be able to shine without lighting it? Just like we reflect Jesus' light, the candle holds the light. Without the fire, there would be no light.

Optional Small Group Chat: Missions Project

This lesson might be a good time to introduce a missions' project to the students.

About the Author:

Pastor Tamera Kraft has been a children's pastor for over thirty years. She is the director of a ministry called Revival Fire For Kids where she mentors other children's leaders, teaches workshops, and is a children's ministry consultant and children's revivalist. She is a recipient of the 2007 National Children's Leaders Association Shepherd's Cup for lifetime achievement in children's ministry.

You can find out more about Revival Fire for Kids at http://revivalfire4kids.net.

www.ingramcontent.com/pod-product-compliance
Lightning Source LLC
Chambersburg PA
CBHW080026130526
44591CB00037B/2685